Modern
Work, P...
Citizenship in Teaching

Modern Times?
Work, Professionalism and Citizenship in Teaching

Martin Lawn

The Falmer Press

(A member of the Taylor & Francis Group)
London • Washington, D.C.

UK The Falmer Press, 1 Gunpowder Square, London, EC4A 3DE
USA The Falmer Press, Taylor & Francis Inc., 1900 Frost Road, Suite 101, Bristol, PA 19007

First published in 1996

A catalogue record for this book is available from the British Library

Library of Congress Cataloging-in-Publication Data are available on request

ISBN 0 7507 0 495 0 cased
ISBN 0 7507 0 496 9 paper

Jacket design by Caroline Archer

Typeset in 10/12pt Garamond by
Graphicraft Typesetters Ltd., Hong Kong.

Printed in Great Britain by Biddles Ltd, Guildford and King's Lynn on paper which has a specified pH value on final paper manufacture of not less than 7.5 and is therefore 'acid free'.

Contents

Acknowledgments

Some of the chapters have been published in earlier versions and have been revised for this book.

1 'The spur and the bridle: Changing the mode of curriculum control', in *Journal of Curriculum Studies*, Vol. 19, no 3, 1987.

2 'The British way and purpose: The spirit of the age in curriculum history', in *Journal of Curriculum Studies*, Vol. 2, no 2, 1989.

3 'A determining moment for teachers: The strike of 1985' was published as 'Teachers' hard lessons' in *Marxism Today*, Vol. 29, no 13, 1985.

4 'The social construction of quality in teaching', in *Evaluation and Research in Education*, 1991.

5 'Encouraging license and insolence in the classroom: Imagining a pedagogic shift', in *Curriculum Studies*, Vol. 3, no 3, 1995.

6 'The end of the modern in teaching?: Implications for professionalism and work', in Kallos, D. and Lindblad, S. (1994) *New Policy Analyses in Education, Sweden and England* University of Umeå Press.

7 'The politics of teaching' was published as 'The political nature of teaching: Arguments around schoolwork', in Ginsberg, M. (Ed) (1995) *The Politics of Educators' Work and Lives*, Garland Press.

The essays contained in this book have been produced over the last ten years and follow through the arguments made in 'Servants of the State' in 1987. They are linked by a need to explore different aspects of teaching, placed within a social and political context, in the last seventy years. They range widely in time and subject and were written for different kinds of mainly academic audiences. With the exception of chapter 1 and chapter 7, they are produced here in the order in which they were written. In different ways, they try to provoke and they are written with more uncertainty in mind than they often display in the text.

I have enjoyed discussion and argument with a number of people who have influenced me, particularly Jenny Ozga, Daniel Kallos and Gerald Grace, and colleagues in the following seminars —

The Comparative Policy Seminar (UK/Sweden) — with thanks to Ingrid Carlgren, Sharon Gewirtz, Sverker Lindblad and Lizbeth Lundahl.

The Umeå University Dept. of Education Seminar.

The AERA Teachers' Work/Teachers' Union Special Interest Group — with thanks to Kari Dehli, Kate Rousmaniere and Harry Smaller.

The Classroom Histories International Seminar — with thanks to Ian Grosvenor.

Introduction

Modern Times? Work, Professionalism and Citizenship in Teaching is about the past in education and the future. It is an attempt to view, from different angles, aspects of the last seventy years of schoolwork, that is the material and social relations of work in school, through a culture/power lens; exploring curriculum, professionalism and unionism, key words of the time, dynamically, within a perspective which emphasizes a struggle over the control and purpose of work in schools.

The use of the term, modern time, is drawn from a set of congruent and interlinked ideas about this period. It combined a fabian organizational style with a conservative approach to self (social) preservation; a project to modernize education as part of an expanding state sector supporting manufacture and commerce; a grand narrative of progress shaped by a particular sense of 'Englishness' and studded with essential myths; a clear sense of a beginning in crisis, a middle of reconstruction and a juddering and sharp end. It is time bound and throughout its evolution and absorption of opposition, it remains distinct. It is physically present in its products; the large buildings of its administrative centres, the colleges for the necessary training, the teacher union's offices and the school spaces (especially and distinctively in the post war period when 8000 primary schools were built). It is present in the policy documents, apologias, public statements and educational writings of the time.

Modern Times? Work, Professionalism and Citizenship in Teaching starts with the premise that the period between the 1920s and the 1990s constitutes a distinct phase in state education which has come to an end. It contained within it the development of a mass public elementary (and later secondary) school system, the establishment of a trained teaching force and the foundation of a local and national public service of education, linked closely to the expansion of state welfare. It is distinct from an earlier phase in which local and national markets in education provided differentiated planes and geographies of schooling containing a variety of teachers and managers labouring in a national vacuum of policy and system in education. The seven decades are distinct in another way, they are permeated by myths. Myths of progress, of national identity and democracy, of professionalism and partnership, of public service and provision. These myths are not untruths but necessary controlling devices, disciplining the employees of the State, and providing reason and identity against other explanations and possibilities. Myths may be generated for one purpose and used for another, they may define an age in such a way that it is difficult to escape their power of explanation. One of the arguments

1

of this book is that commonsense understandings and theoretical interpretations in education may still rely upon the mythological features of the past, particularly professionalism, to obscure the breaks between the 1990s and the previous, dominant phase of education.

One way to recognize the past is to compare it with the present, something many commentators did unfavourably in the late 1980s when the conservative reforms came blustering into place. The initial shock of rapid and accumulating educational change has now receded in England even though its after effects continue to disrupt schools and teachers. The imposition of the curriculum and assessment reforms, new inspection systems and decentralized management on people and their work altered the education landscape. Quantitatively, in each school, there were immediate effects on hours of work, resources, subject and pedagogical skills, followed by search for solutions to organizational problems. Qualitatively, new kinds of problems emerged in the social relations of work; initially, they were in the new kinds of management of people and tasks that were needed in the school and then they widened to include the ways that teachers managed each other. The rippling effects of the national reforms in schools had the same consequences for schoolwork as a major restructuring of an industry in the 1990s would have on all its employees. This is most clearly seen in the parallels and homologies which can be drawn between the way new industries or businesses work and the way schools now appear to work. A similar language is used in both places, emphasizing quality, human resources, management cycles, teams of specialist staff, flexibilities of operation, focussing of resources etc. This language may be only a surface feature or it may be a sign of significant changes in work. Similarities between schools and other forms of enterprise can be found either because they are operating under the same improvement programmes (such as Investors in People) or because in a quasi market similarities will outweigh differences.

The initial language of shock used by teachers emphasized the lack of care used in the implementation of reform, teacher overwork and lack of communication about programmes and policies. However for education commentators and academics the reforms signified the symbolic end of a period in education which had become a kind of cultural commonsense among educationalists. The disruptive or imported nature of the curriculum reform was seen as a particularly strong intervention in the history and culture of education in England. When it was linked with a decentralization of power away from the elected local authorities, the reforms cut across the dominant descriptions and ideological formation of the education service. That had been seen, mythologized, as a partnership between units of equal power, the centre, the local and the teachers; the curriculum and its determination was based upon this power relation and so could not be seen as an imposition on teachers. A national curriculum, devised without teachers and imposed upon them, was regarded as a severe breach of etiquette, possibly a major infringement of rights and certainly as a break with the past. In these responses can be found the significance of the reforms. They are both a major restructuring of teachers' work and a significant break with the previously dominant discourse about the education system in England.

The idea of a break with the past was commonly present in the arguments of the late 1980s. As the shock of the reform interventions wore off, to be replaced by innovation fatigue and constant reorganization, it was replaced by the creation of new mythologies. In these mythologies, the market replaced the government and the public service; management replaced partnership; planning replaced responsibility. The past was now clearly in relief, defensively placed as the time when the education system was inadequate, not concerned with improvement and obsessed with equality.

This book is about that past, a past seen less simply here. It is seen as associated with the rise of the ideas of professionalism and partnership in education, with the growth of social democratic policies and planning and the extension of the public services. Significant features of this period were the complexity and sophistication of the ways in which public servants were managed and controlled, the interweaving of industrial solutions into educational sites and the consolidation of the work of teaching. In education, the work of schools was defined steadily and teaching had a degree of stability in its operation and representation. Active citizenship by teachers and pupils appeared to define the creation and the processes of the school curriculum. As a distinct phase in the education service in England, it is being treated within this book as partly chronological, roughly from the 1920s to the 1980s, even though it came into existence in different significant ways from the earliest decade of the century and that its personnel and leaders stayed within its service in the 1990s. It begins with visions of the future, plans for implementation, public interest and manoeuvrings around control[1]; discourse and regulation begin to form and are used and opposed. The place of teachers as full citizens, able to rationalize their place and identity, inquire into their work and argue about its purpose and praxis, organize to change, encourage others to join and work with the grain of a reconstructing and socializing society are the hallmarks of the time as it is represented and as it might have been. The end of modernity, as these essays imply, comes when the discourse, the forms of control, its drive and confidence, are eroded. The material and ideological conditions which are to be derived from or shaped by quasi market discourse create new kinds of disciplines of work but exclude claims to active citizenship and the external social spheres of work (which social movements were interweaved with). The old legitimacies of professionalism are subdued by new presumptions about work, its costs, its management and organization.

However, the debate about modernism in education can't be reduced to questions of chronological time, and the way it is to be treated here varies. The essays in this book deal with different aspects of the education system since the 1920s, looking at how the system was generated and grew, the myths and icons which were used to represent it and the spaces within it where oppositional and fluid social movements could act. However the tentative and questioning nature of the idea, expressed in the title, is used deliberately not only to suggest a powerful descriptor of a distinctive time in education yet to allow for ambiguity within an analysis which has moved from a critical engagement with the period, looking for oppositional or historically invisible agencies to a recognition that the silences and invisibilities extended to teachers and their work.[2]

These essays concentrate on the social construction of the modern teacher. The struggle occurs over a number of terrains, in various and sometimes contradictory ways. This makes the inquiry nearer to cultural studies than to history of education. What is being explored here are aspects of the culture and politics of teaching in the mid-twentieth century to reveal the submerged movements by teachers and others to define teaching within modernity. Immersed in classrooms, social movements and unions; operating in staffrooms, committee meetings and publication; interacting in a range of social, educational and political arenas: teachers tried to construct their identities as teachers. The social construction of the modern teacher took place against images and possible identities and determining conditions which could not be avoided. It was the idea of the teacher as much as the practice of teaching that was the object of this endeavour. It was constructed against others by sex, work or class as much as for a positive identity. The modern teacher was not a stable construction, it had contradictions within itself, but it was created in the making.

This book is made up of a series of essays which were produced as part of a consistent project on the histories of the curriculum, politics, professionalism and unions in schooling, in the span of a decade. These essays constitute evidence and argument about this particular phase of English education. This argument is about a distinctive project in which the construction of the modern teacher within the formation and extension of a mass education system was undertaken, opposed and developed. The argument is about the ways in which this project worked; through conditions of work, myths and controls. The argument accumulates in these essays about the project; different cases illuminate the ways in which teaching was constructed. Teachers are explored in a number of ways, in contrasting sources and with diverse questions: they are seen within unions, as the object of management controls, within policy documents on recruitment, in strikes, in staffrooms and logbooks. The angle and the purpose are varied. The articulation of the transformation of teaching needs a variety of approaches to develop a complexity of interpretation. There is no straight forward narrative of progress or even of struggle but a series of engagements, perspectives and processes in which the ideas and structures of the phase may be seen and heard. Sometimes reporting the activity of the teachers was taken as an end in itself, in other essays, the concern was with power and control, moving from the idea of indirect rule or the colonizing of teachers to their central role in the modernization of schooling and back again to the idea of an organizational narrative which rendered them invisible.

Although a thesis about the end of a phase in education raises questions about difference, there is also a set of themes in these essays which suggest similarities. The politics and techniques of control is one theme. Others include curriculum change, the creation of legitimating myths, the relation between innovation and teachers' work. The tension between pedagogy and system change is an issue as well. As the essays take on diverse subjects, they juxtapose information, subjects, time, angles and point of view so that they can be read as a form of montage, resonating on several levels at once.[3]

Also the theorizing and expression of the essays differs throughout the book. This is partly due to the way I approached and constructed the problems shifted in the decade in which they were produced. This is a low-tech response to major shifts in theorizing associated with post structuralism, post fordism and post modernism and the recognition of the way I appeared to be unconsciously using or even driving the modernizing discourse in my arguments. The shift from a critique, even an implied one, of an event or an idea to a reproduction of the fundamental discourse of modernization is not as great as I assumed it would have been when I started out and which now in retrospect I can see that it is. The essay, 'A determining moment for teachers: The strike of 1985', was written as a description of the past and as a guide to the future. The latter was never my strong point and so I didn't expect it to last but it is the ideas of the first part which I have concerned myself with since. The historical work which it was supported by I still acknowledge, although the strength of the narrative drive and force of its theoretical position I could not now reproduce so confidently. For example, the use of the concept of partnership, popular in the controlling myths of the time, does not appear to be used ironically but only tactically when I contrast different control strategies against each other for interpretive advantage. While legitimate perhaps, a dominant metaphor devised for teachers is used which is unknowingly controlling the writer. The historical difficulties for the left in opposing the State often co-existed with the problems of improving it. Opposition and improvement were often encased, at this time, in some of the same presuppositions that they opposed, leaving the argument to be waged through resources, legitimacy and scope. My consistent emphasis on the teacher in the school, the union and in social movements was used to force a recognition of the complexity of teachers' work in the analysis of education. Ironically, over time this left less emphasis on the visibility/invisibility of teachers.

The essays in this book involve different kinds of historical inquiry and critical writing. They are quite argumentative and polemical yet they do rest upon a consistent attempt to either unpick key elements of the modernist project in education, particularly professionalism, improvement, autonomy and teacher education. In later essays, shifts in teachers' work and the place of teacher unions are scrutinized in relation to the past and the problems of the present. The past is receding fast and many of the illusory and myth bearing aspects of this period, which once reigned supreme, have been obliterated even though I argue that they continue within the residual culture of education, cut off from their roots.

One of the facets of the modern time in education was a concern for control over teachers. The very idea of teachers being a social danger is still around, through moral panics or right wing restorationist polemics on training or the curriculum, but not to the same degree it was in the 1920s. Progressive policy on education, Labour modernization programmes and broadly reformative liberal, socialist and feminist ideas among teachers were viewed by conservatives as a threat to the State and the natural order of society. Re-establishing control over teachers began in several ways, particularly through the ideology of professionalism within the broader idea of an 'English' system of educational governance. It is this pervading myth which is still seen to have analytical value even though its use value is eroded by the emergence of new forms of work controls. This 'English' approach depended upon the creation of a new model of the teacher, able to recognize their new duty, within a democracy, which came to be seen more and more as the creation of young citizens. The responsibilities of the teacher within the system of education and within the school was expressed as a partnership (with local and national government), as professionalism and as a curriculum autonomy.

Another facet was the way in which employees in the system of education used these ideas, meant to control them, and turned them into bargaining tools or oppositional capacities. Partnership, professionalism and autonomy came to have complex meanings. It was necessary to understand the context in which they were used, by whom and which place and time. A third aspect of the time is the obscuring of the actual work of the schools and the other particular spaces of the system by the power of the mythology about their workings. Possible reconstructions of the way in which schools worked, the way in which teachers might be created to perform in those schools and the oppositional behaviours they may have exhibited are minimal.

The opening essay, the 'Politics of Teaching: Arguments Around School-work' serves as a general introduction to the main contention of the book, that a modern period of education in England, associated with the expansion and rebuilding of state education, was a distinctive period in the formation of teaching, structurally, ideologically and professionally. It was distinctive in its politicization of teaching in a number of ways even though it may look as if politics were excluded from teaching. Its distinctiveness lies in its peculiar 'English' methods of control through symbols, regulation and myth. Endemic to this process was the managing of 'independence'; paradoxically, 'independence' meant control. Indeed key defining terms, in this period, such as 'profession', were reinvented and deployed to manage and control teachers. This essay touches upon the other emerging feature of this period, the oppositional and influential actions of teachers, creating their own movements and political/educational projects. The complexities of the time have to be unravelled: the search to pacify, incorporate and manage teachers in the modern project of mass schooling was mirrored by the positional, pervading and unconstraining response of teachers. Contested tactical and strategic plans about work and ciizenship were mixed with alliances about means or ends in the development of an education system. Winning support for immediate disputes, short term political advantage and overall hegemony was constant. Teachers had to be managed differently to other groups of workers; in the modernizing of schools, they were crucial but they always had the potential to be a social danger to the State.

The essays are loosely organized chronologically, moving through the modern period. 'The Spur and the Bridle' is an exploration of the way in which indirect control of teachers replaced direct control; it acts as an explanation of the 1920s, a commentary on the end of this system in the 1980s and as a reproof to the 1990s. 'Modernizing Professionalism' views the actions of radical teachers in the 1920s as opponents of the State and the object of its concerns, as the key reforming generation of teachers in the post-war decades and the forerunners of a recent form of teacher-based inquiry.

The 'British Way and Purpose' is an essay about curriculum change; how social crisis produces radical reform, new tools of change are created and teachers are influenced by social ideas and use new forms of pedagogy. It is a counterpoint to a curriculum history which reads teacher power, in their subject associations, as the standard arena of change and excludes social crises, adversarial actions and radical purpose.

'Social Constructions of Quality in Teaching' is a study of the consistent attempt, by the State, to define and shape teachers for schools and shows how the definition of the 'good teacher' altered according to the labour markets for skilled workers, the need for a compliant and differentially skilled work-force and the redefinition of state purposes, related to structural changes or ideological shifts in the education system. The social construction of teacher quality is a contested process, both management and teachers engaged with current definitions of the 'good teacher'.

'Encouraging License and Insolence in the Classroom' strives to explore the puzzle of pedagogical change. The discussion method was closely associated with the rise of new school subjects or activities, such as civics and social studies, the shift to a practical curriculum and teacher autonomy and responsibility. The concept of discussion is characteristic of this period, a recurring theme in the writings about schools in the 1950s, yet it is difficult to track. Did it really exist at all?

'A Determining Moment for Teachers' was a commentary on the teachers' disputes in the mid-1980s with an attempt to register their significance as the beginning of the end of the modern period, its ways of working and mythologies. The essay is itself a period artefact, working in and against the suppositions of the times; it explained the significance of the dispute against the past, reads as a clear oppositional narrative, and yet is dependent on the use of the same modern icons as partnership and professionalism. Even though it is too harsh in its judgments it still makes sense about the crisis in which new forms of management of teachers were emerging.

'Reform Dilemmas for the Union' explores contemporary teacher unions through their changing roles, continuing effectiveness and future use value in the quasi market in schooling. Of specific interest is the relation between school reform and unions. The labour process of teaching, and its underlying rationale (in teaching, ideas on learning and pedagogy, classroom organization, support structures etc), is affected by reform but in ways which a defensive organization finds difficult to do more than resist or try to avoid. School reform has the same potential as changing the production line or redesigning the office. It is worth trying to analyse the shifts needed in England in teacher unions which are seen as vital to reform; this is explicit in the USA but often implicit in England.

'The End of the Modern in Teaching?' surveys the changes in teachers' work since the 1988 Education Act and the consequences of the move away from the way education was organized, described and worked in the post-war period. Through the tension between progressive social and education policies many teachers supported, and the delivery of a labour process which controlled and tried to determine them, I look at the association of particular kinds of labour processes with the post-war rise of modern schooling and secondly, try and discern the implications for teachers of the new labour processes emerging after the 1988 Education Act.

'Second Guessing the Past' is a paper about the key factors in teacher unionism — context, identity, contradiction, competition and work organization — which shape teachers' professional associations and an exploration of the courses of action open to teacher unions, within the context of regulation and market.

'Orderings and Disorderings' explores the significance of the post-war public service and the recent restructuring for a school and analyses the substantive versus superficial changes which have occurred in the school in recent years and the confusions which have arisen about its work and context.

Together these essays are intended to illuminate the public troubles of the public system of schooling in its distinctive modern phase, the 1920s to the 1980s.

Notes

1 For me, it is located in the words and actions of the work of Eustace Percy, the work of Beatrice and Sydney Webb and the Teachers' Labour League, and writers (like Wells, Cole and Neill) and it was sustained by many others in later years from the teacher associations, local authorities and all sites of teacher education.
2 *Invisible* agencies is not a metaphysical notion but is intended to draw attention to the lack of inquiry in the history of education to these areas, substantively and methodologically.
3 A contention about form influenced by Pred (1995) and the idea of montage.

1 The Politics of Teaching: Arguments Around Schoolwork

In this chapter, I begin by explaining my use of the terms, 'politics and teachers', in relation to each other and in particular with regard to the study of teachers' work *as work*, the creation of policy related to the conditions and contexts of work and the right of teachers to be involved in the creation and maintenance of that policy. Secondly, I describe the early formation in the modern period of a distinctive way of managing teachers, their work and their politics by their incorporation into the education system (using the ideas of Sydney Webb [1918]) and the management of their 'independence' under indirect rule. The consequence of these congruent processes was the paradox for the politics of teaching that teachers had to be non-political. Thirdly, I raise another related issue about teacher politics, which was the social danger the teaching workforce represented to the modern State. Even though this danger might be symbolic, it had consequences for the political relations between teachers and the State. The social danger of an organized teacher workforce wasn't necessarily based on what teachers did, it was what they represented. However, while the danger might be symbolic, the means to deal with the collective of political teachers also included a method of policing the boundaries of teaching so that they became separated and coerced. Fourthly, I explore the continuing politics of teaching in the modern period as a war of position, based around the double-edged ideology of professionalism, around schoolwork disputes and around images of the 'good' teacher. Finally, I want to look at a further and related aspect of the relations between the State and teachers. Each party had to win support politically over time, in periods of change. Teachers might work within teaching as part of their membership of new social movements. They work, in and outside of their unions, in a discrete public politics which involves the policies of the State and contemporary ideas about work, citizenship and society and which is affected by different periods in the development of the modern State.

Politics and Work

I should begin by explaining my use of the term 'political' with regard to teachers' beliefs and actions. I am interested in the way teachers act politically within education, acting within their teacher associations and making alliances with other groups or using a language of politics drawn from outside teaching to explore their roles, relations and work.[1] I am also interested in the way the modern State (using England and Wales as an example of the modern social democratic State in the twentieth century) deals with its workforce of teachers politically.

My argument about teachers and politics is based on the assumption that teachers have certain legitimate interests which flow out of their conditions of work: these interests seem to cross all kinds of societies if they employ a distinct group of people in a system of schooling. Teaching is organized in the modern State within particular forms of production, containing labour processes which determine many aspects of the content, skills, speed and work relations of teaching. This is not a socially neutral process to be excluded from our understanding of what teaching is; without a knowledge of the work context of teaching, their collective actions, in their various forms tend to make little sense or are excluded by nature of their lack of fit to the 'real' teaching. As the school is a site of struggle over the nature of teaching so is the history of the relations between the teachers and their employers; in one form or another this means the State in modern democratic societies. As has been argued before:

> The study of teachers' work as work should remain at the centre of research in this area. Like other forms of work, teaching should be properly served by a thorough study of its practices, struggles, lived experience and contradictions. Such an approach can range from studies of relations at work or the politics of skill control through to local and national policy-making involving organised teachers and their arguments on the nature of their industry. Most importantly, this study should be historical, recognising the movement of teachers in and out of teaching, and change in schools, in local authorities and in central and local educational policies. (Ozga and Lawn, 1988, p. 334)

Obviously the concerns of the collective of teachers are expressed within their organized deliberations, as is their relationship with their employer and management. Another feature of their work is their interest in the policies reflected in the schooling system, viz., its funding, expansion or decline, resources, current ideologies. Yet when teachers involve themselves in these policy areas it can be regarded by their local and national employers as a usurpation of 'democratic' processes or the management's right to manage. Teachers can be seen as both main agents of social reproduction *and* low status operatives in the education system: this is the source of the contradiction which the phrase 'the political nature of teaching' describes. It is revealed in different ways, for example, in the gap between their actions and the way these actions are seen by the State. Alternatively, this tension in their work and their relations with the State is seen in contemporary English history within debates on professionalism, following a strike or an outbreak of moral panic or a political crisis. This tension may very well take different forms in other societies, it will always be there in one form or another. So politics means, in this context, the achievement of policy related to the conditions and contexts of work *and* the right to be involved in policy making.

However, this right to be involved in policy making leads into a further dimension of teacher politics. Teachers aren't neutral in society or just defenders of their labour process. They may enter into teaching with a particular view of society and education, expressed within contemporary politics or social movements. They may develop a social/education project which leads them into a party or movement membership or into public alliances through their collective associations.

When a new group or class is beginning to move towards power, it must develop support and then win hegemony. In the twentieth century in particular, teachers are important, locally and nationally, as key members of the community and/or workers in a key public service. In this situation teachers are both the audience (the potential support) and often part of the new group attempting to win power and so are often politically involved. They may be divided sometimes by gender, race or school sector (elementary and secondary) in their attraction to this form of politics and its solutions to their problems.

In Nazi Germany, for example, many teachers moved into the Nazi party when they were faced with a deprofessionalization process which attacked their standard of living and their role as cultural agents. Using Nazi arguments about women and Jews in their profession, they tried to exclude them. Moreover, 'they facilitated the erosion of Weimar democracy and turned youths towards illiberalism' (Jarausch, 1985, p. 394). Yet in Britain, a decade earlier, the early rise of the Labour Party attracted teachers as voters or members, partly because it offered a new professionalism, a role in policy making and better pay.[2] Teachers may also be used by groups hoping to retain hegemony. Both the Left and the Right may view teachers as possible agents in the creation of a new society: in effect this always meant that certain groups of teachers were favoured, while others were expelled.

There are also permanent political tensions around the job of teaching which surface in times of crisis or when a radical government is organized. A statement like this one, made by a *préfet* in Vichy France, can echo around any society:

> The National Revolution will never really penetrate the countryside except through the teachers: if the Government has at its disposal a body of primary schoolteachers who are attached to the regime and who are the leading propagandists of its doctrine, the rural masses will be all but won over. (Kedward and Austin, 1985, p. 16)

The Vichy question is always there, expressed in different ways in different places, and its result is that teachers find out that trying to change their work or even just keeping quiet involves politics. If they aren't trying to alter their work somebody else will: there is no stasis in the policy and management of education and teaching!

These elements, such as the language of confrontation or responsibility, the greater or lesser concern with social and political loyalty, the generally low status and high social responsibility, the changing idea of the State with its major restructuring or creation of new education sectors may vary at different times in different societies. What is consistent is the tension between teachers and their employers revealed in the working out of these elements and the social/education projects, expressed within party or movement membership. This is the source of the public politics of teaching.

Four examples reveal the complexity of this public politics. Firstly, Nikkyoso, the main teachers' organization in Japan has a constitution which defines the teacher as a labourer albeit one who defends freedom, equal opportunity and proper government. This is a reflection of its opposition to the old imperial idea of the teacher and the influence of the post-war US administration. This idea, deeply embedded in its definition of its own union-ized 'good teachers', has now to be persistently defended against a State which has moved conservatively to absorb the older ideas of the imperial State and to reject the Nikkyoso model. Interestingly, divisions occurred in the union when the Socialist Party faction opposed the suggestion (from the Communist Party) that the older definition of the teacher as part of a 'sacred profession,' associated with the proscription of strikes and political activity among teach-ers, should be re-introduced. So, again, professionalism is introduced and, in this case, is used to divide teachers and expressed within different party alle-giances or factions which, presumably, follow a party line in the union. As one of its tactics for defence Nikkyoso sponsors a large annual research conference to further its foundation aims to establish a democratic education system and freedom of research and it tries to make alliances with groups of education-alists or citizens in the wider society (Ota, 1985).

Secondly, in Portugal the post-revolutionary teacher unions began to use the idea of professionalism to defend teachers from attacks by a Conservat-ive Government wishing to 'normalize' schooling, though unions attached to either the Communist or Socialist/Social Democratic Party used this term in different ways. Indeed different unions organize themselves around key polit-ical and educational ideas which distinguish them from the other unions and take them nearer or farther away from the government. These ideas are fun-damental and represent the teachers' own views and involvement in a chang-ing Portugal, allying them with other groups of workers in their associations (Stoer, 1985). Thirdly, the Maltese teacher union was influenced by the Catho-lic Church and opposed to the secular, independence leaders, the Labour Party (Darmanin, 1985). It found itself on political and cultural grounds unable to work with an independent Labour government which in turn, was unable to develop any strategies to win hegemony in education without teachers. Fourthly, in Jamaica, both teacher unions supported political independence, partly to increase their influence over policy-making and particularly to encourage the 'nationalization' of the elementary schools, though they did not affiliate dir-ectly to the new parties (Goulbourne, 1988). Anti-colonial independence movements may cause difficulties for unions created as a reflection of a colonial system of education.

The Making of Modern Teachers in Britain

In the modern period of state education in Britain, which in my view extends from the early 1920s to the late 1970s, a dependable corps of teachers was important to the State and its parties in the creation of a new, mass education system. This political concern with dependability translated itself into a practical philosophy of teacher management and an ideology of professionalism which shaped what teachers should or would be doing in their social behaviour and work relations. The modern British State, this century, was influenced, firstly, by a social democratic Labour Party which saw teachers as a crucial part of the government of education. This view of the essentially political nature of teaching has its roots in a paper by Sydney Webb, the Fabian theorist, written in 1918, at a time when popular education was expanding and the Labour Party was trying to encourage teachers to join. Webb (1918) argued that:

> as systematic education is now more and more predominantly a Government function, and the bulk of the teaching profession is enrolled in one or other form of public service, we have necessarily to treat all educational projects as being, in the strictest sense of the word, politics, and as politics of the highest national importance . . . [The teaching profession] has consequently a claim to exercise a professional judgement, to formulate distinctive opinions upon its own and upon cognate services, and to enjoy its own appropriate share in the corporate government of its own working life. (Webb, 1918, p. 3)

In policy terms Webb (1918, pp. 4–6) argued that teachers should 'advise and warn, to initiate and criticise, but not decide'. The claim to a political role for teachers then was based on a new claim to professional service for all the community, regardless of the 'affluence or status of the persons in need', and the means and organization for this to be achieved. It should instruct those who 'move for educational reform what exactly it is that they should demand and press for'. This was an invitation to policy making by the front door and was the herald of a shift in state policy towards teachers and a bid to win teachers over to a new hegemony by Labour.

The second influence on the State in its relation to its teachers was the generation of a distinctive way of managing teachers, drawn from British colonial practice, which depended on the discreet use of power, control of finance and a dominant ideology of self-government. At the same time as Webb was developing his view on the essentially political nature of teaching, an important Minister of Education, Eustace Percy, argued with members of his own Conservative Party that the leftward drift of the teachers (in the 1920s) should not be met with an overt attack upon them by means of oaths of allegiance to the State, but that 'the best safeguard against [the drift of teachers towards the labour party etc.] is to give teachers a sense of reasonable independence and not to subordinate them too much either to a central or to a local authority' (Lawn, 1987a, p. 119). This idea of a 'reasonable independence' soon developed into a major political myth, coming to characterize the distinctly British, democratic way of governance, particularly in the education service, against totalitarian systems in the 1930s through to the 1960s. So, in effect, the social democratic incorporation of teachers into the management of the service and the conservative approach to managing education were homologous (although not entirely).

What is not evident in the statement by Webb is the other part of the bargain to be struck with teachers. If teaching was political, in the sense of being part of the corporate governance of the education system, then teachers had to become non-political, another paradox. This paradox is present in the theory of teaching professionalism expounded by Asher Tropp in the 1950s. Tropp argued that the teachers' union was determinedly non-political but operated a series of alliances, discarded at the union's convenience, with political parties or other significant groups to achieve its consistent aims. In his view, the profession of teaching:

> was created by the state and in the [nineteenth century] the state was powerful enough to claim almost complete control over the teacher and to manipulate his [or her] status while at the same time disclaiming all responsibility towards him [or her]. Slowly, and as the result of prolonged effort, the organized profession has won free and has reached a position of self-government and independence. (Tropp, 1957, p. 4)

It may be summarized in this way: the more non-political the union was, the more power it was able to achieve or was given and as long as non-political meant non-party political, then, it was possible for the unions to talk of professionalism. Because of the new importance of education to the State, and of teachers within the management of the education system, the politics of teaching meant that teachers had to be non-political. The main question in England was how best this was to be achieved.

Policing the Boundary

One consequence of this modern definition of the teacher, as non-political and as an independent professional, is the way in which the world of teaching is defined so that any attempt to view the teacher outside the frame of the classroom is seen as unnatural. While this approach places teachers at the centre of the frame, it does so by reducing the teacher; they are shorn of the political, economic and cultural aspects of their work. This is not just a comment on the paucity of theoretical understandings about teachers, constantly separating these aspects from some version of the core teacher, it is a reflection of the dominant way in which teachers are managed. Paradoxically, one of the ways the political nature of teaching is dramatically acknowledged by the State is when there is a moral panic about the politics of teachers and what they may do and may not do in the classroom and in society. The history of teaching, prior to the 1920s, suggests that the fact that teachers existed as a group was enough for them to be regarded suspiciously by political leaders. It wasn't what they did; it was what they represented. Historically, they were seen as a problem when they either grew in numbers so that the guardians of the State felt they were either (1) out of control and becoming too secular (i.e., disruptive of the natural order because of their existence!); (2) expressing their opinion about their work, however discreetly, in a way which their employers found challenging, or (3) using a language or taking actions which appeared to link them to a wider labour movement. What appears to count was the *symbolic* nature of their actions not the reality of the action itself. It was what their teachers *appeared* to be doing!

As their numbers grew, teachers were regarded collectively as a possible social danger. This perspective on teachers by their local employers (members of the business class, the landed class or the Church), expressed in local discussions on teachers' pay, or by contemporary observers in the national press concerned about their political or social influence, should not be ignored. It is not that teachers' actual political views or actions were extreme, in the main, but the fear their actions cause and the symbolic power they are seen as wielding to a State concerned with control or reproduction. While the political beliefs of some teachers were regarded as a reason not to employ them and these teachers were a numerical minority, their presence caused outrage among the ruling elite (Lawn, 1987a).

The modern response of an indirect control and professionalism was a sophisticated way of managing the social danger of the teaching workforce. To manage the collectivity of apolitical teachers, within this corral of a limited independence, it was necessary to police the boundaries. In this operation action was used against individuals and loudly publicized to 'encourage the others'! The policing generally operated through teacher politics scares, involving bans and proscription as well as local campaigns against individual teachers and unions. At the same time the local and national press pursued individual teachers, while statements about professionalism were made in conferences or in public meetings by ministers to isolate radicals or freethinkers from the rest. Teachers were sacked in the 1920s for their beliefs, which in a time of teacher unemployment must have been very effective in reducing the idea of teacher politics to a question of private belief and quiet party membership. In the 1940s and early 1950s there was a ban on teacher membership of the Communist Party in parts of London.

In later years, it was union membership that was regarded as a sign of external forces, symbolically and practically, intruding into the natural relations between the employer and the employee. The union officer or union lawyer arriving to help members in a dispute was always the herald for an outcry about 'our teachers and outside agitators'.[3] They were seen to represent an outside force which attempts to destroy the harmony of work relations locally (Ozga, 1987). It is a major political act to be a school building representative of a teachers' union and could be described, in the past, as attempting to 'turn the world upside down'. This suggests that a 'natural' world is broken when teachers are seen as threatening the local status quo; politics and work are easily joined in this symbol of disruption.

Schoolwork: The Social Construction of the Good Teacher

The incorporation of teachers into the modern idea of the non-political servant of the State needed policing at its boundaries and a regular reinforcement of the ideology. The ideology of professionalism operated at a number of levels; versions of a General Teaching Council, regular pronouncements about teacher professionalism from ministers, consultations at local and national level, membership of advisory bodies, etc. But, professionalism is a double-edged sword. As well as being a way of controlling teachers, it can be used to protect the space around the labour process in the arena of policy and politics. Professionalism becomes part of the politics of the labour process, a political notion which teachers and their unions have drawn upon to defend schoolwork or to demand access to change. Professionalism was a major weapon in their tactics but it is a sensitive one; the State is capable of using it itself, of dividing teachers by it and of restructuring education so that it is of reduced value. The use of professionalism by teachers and the State is one arena for political manoeuvring around the politics of teaching in England and Wales. An example of this is the way that a strike or a dispute could be regarded as a professional action by some teachers, unprofessional by other teachers as well as by the government.

Another arena is schoolwork, the labour process of teaching where teachers, like other people, try to determine the nature of their work through individual and collective action to structure work relations at the school site in the context of national and local policies. The social construction of skill is a powerful tool, but it comes from a particular 'kit,' and needs to be located in labour process theory. . . . Labour process theory provides the theoretical framework, and the social construction of skill is a key component of the labour process of teaching. This emphasis puts the politics of the production process in schools — something recognized by current governments — in higher profile. In teaching, active agency and therefore teacher politics are key elements of the labour process . . . The labour process perspective outlined here clarifies the intentions of the State in controlling its educational workforce, but also permits us to more fully understand individual teachers' tactical and strategic actions (Lawn and Ozga, 1988, p. 334).

Schoolwork is not just an internal school process or a union one. One of the ways this war of position is seen is through the definition of the 'good teacher', that is the image of the teacher on which educational policy makers or managers have created expectations for teachers is based.[4] Teaching quality is seen here as a social construction, an attempt to make visible and explicit the practical and ideological management imperatives in any given period. There tend to be competing definitions of the 'good teacher'. The social construction of teacher quality is a contested process; initiatives are taken in response to shortages or emerge out of particular political and social conjunctions which are then responded to by teachers. In turn, teachers produce their own versions of the 'good teacher', using the contradictions of particular times and places, and influenced by wider ideas moving through society. Generations of teachers are themselves divided, containing as they do, competing practices, favoured 'good teacher' models and biographically ordered work experience around which teachers organize or group.

So, this version of politics has to be seen contextually. It reflects a particular shift in the place of education versus the State. The role of the teacher differs from society to society and from period to period. The definition of the 'good teacher' must then differ as the State decides the role the employed teacher should take through a training, management or inspection process. For example, the 'good teacher' was defined as an active citizen and the educator of other active citizens-to-be in Britain after the Second World War; the reconstruction of the new society was seen, in part, as the responsibility of the teacher and so the 'good teacher union' was expected to play a major role in the new system (Lawn, 1987b). Indeed, these definitions of the 'good teacher' and the 'good teacher union' were an extension of the 'reasonable independence' teacher, a symbol of the organizing myths of the modern period, given some actuality in the period of post-war reconstruction under a Labour Government.

Teacher unionism has political aspects when it is actively engaging with the labour process in school (schoolwork). In England today this could mean defending pedagogy, questioning curriculum content, opposing performance appraisal and the dismantling of teacher training. In the past, it meant campaigning for child welfare policies and a comprehensive schooling system. Teacher unionism is political when it seeks alliances to achieve major policy changes in national programmes or structures — for example, on vocational education — with employers or other unions.

The current English definition of the 'good teacher', a 1980s post-modern definition in my terms, is nearer to that of competent employee, trying to meet production or efficiency targets, decided nationally and rewarded locally. In this case the 'good teacher union' has an impossible role, expected to be active by its members and inactive by the State. Far from an encouragement to be active citizens, restrictions are now operating on their civil liberties with regard to standing for school governorships and local councils. So, what is viewed as political by the employee or the employer will vary according to the dominant definition of the 'good teacher' of the particular period.

Social Movements and the Politics of Teaching

There is a further expression of the teachers and politics question. When a new group or class is beginning to move towards power, it must develop support and then win hegemony. In the twentieth century in particular, teachers are important, locally and nationally, as key members of the community and/or workers in a key public service. In this situation teachers are both the audience (the potential support) and often part of the new group attempting to win power, and so are often politically involved. They may be divided sometimes by gender, race or school sector (elementary and secondary) in their attraction to this form of politics and its solutions to their problems. Both the Left and the Right may view teachers as possible agents in the creation of a new society. In effect, this has always meant that groups of teachers were favoured while others were made outsiders.

In England, there have been, historically, at least two examples of the connection between teachers and social movements. One is the relation between teachers and the labour movement in the early decades of the century, where it is clear that teachers acted as resources for local movements of socialists of various kinds and for emerging unions. The early rise of the Labour Party attracted teachers as voters or members, partly because it offered a new professionalism, a role in policy making and better pay. Teachers may also be used by groups hoping to retain hegemony. 'The Drift of Teachers to the Labour Party', as the political police (the Special Branch) called it, occurred in the early 1920s and there are cases recorded of waves of disgruntled teachers working hard at election time for Labour Party candidates (Lawn, 1987a). In rural areas teachers had been involved with the organization of farm worker unions. This connection grew over the years so that significant groups of teachers were active in left-wing causes in the following decades.

The second significant link is between women teachers and the first wave feminism of the suffragettes. This resulted in the creation of a new union, the National Union of Women Teachers, in the early 1920s which united the feminist teachers of the period, many of whom had been in the suffrage movement (Lawn, 1987a). They were described recently as subjugating themselves to the cause of feminism:

> Their identity as feminists was forged through an adherence to the greater political cause, of which each individual was a part. This concept of feminist identity also helped them make sense of their role as educators inside — and outside — the classroom. (Kean, 1990, p. 45)

Another writer described these teachers as being part of a 'vigorous, optimistic feminist network' (King, 1987, p. 32). So, the relation between teachers and wider social movements is complex, suggesting an interplay between politics, social movements and teachers' work which is possibly more interesting than organized alliances.

Recent debates about the emergence of new social movements (NSMs) in Britain, such as feminism, the peace movement and the green alliance, have raised questions about the role of the service class and, in particular, professional public service employees in their formation. In sum, it is suggested that the growth of the service class is related to the rise of new political agendas and organizations and the restructuring of old class relations. A part of this argument, which may illuminate the political role of teachers, suggests that public employees 'facilitate the emergence of new social movements through the application of their skills as producers and organizers of knowledge' (Bagguley, 1992, p. 39). The same author suggests that this class has two areas of political practice; the first is a form of professional trade unionism, often involving the State as employer, and the second is in civil society, locally based, where they act as a resource for social movements, conservative or progressive.

This then suggests that teachers may be seen as political actors more clearly elsewhere than in their unions *and* that a union may act as a vehicle to express these wider social and political activities. When teachers were the only educated members of the community and were working in the public service, they had an influence in other ways (in Britain and elsewhere).

> [Teachers] could use their cultural capital locally by acting as 'experts' in different fields, such as hygiene, vaccination, gardening, local administration, etc.; and their training also gave them cultural competence to lead choirs, theatricals, to form associations and lead courses. Teachers occupied a key position in local communities. (Florin, 1987, p. 196)

Political action, built on a local cultural role, is a powerful one. From the turn of the century, in England, there was a growing concern among the elite about the political and social effect of teachers acting as political agents. When the Labour Party grew and began to attract teachers with its educational and social policies, concern was palpable in the ruling elite. Teachers were not and are not an homogenous group, they are recruited from different social classes, for different school sectors, in different periods. It is not surprising, therefore, that their political action should take different forms or that the State should operate in awareness of their role both as agents and resisters.

Conclusion

I would suggest that teachers may be seen as political actors because of their conditions of work and their own views and actions, individually or collectively, on their work. Their role as political actors has particular meaning in a social democratic project, especially one like England's, where there is an expectation of working in and for the State as a public employee and at the same time a particular way of managing employees of the State. The consequence of this 'indirect rule' and an ideology of independence is the circumvention of teachers' political action. A sort of professional welfarism ensued in which only a favourable apoliticism by the teachers was allowed. The social danger that teachers symbolized was neutered by co-optation.

In this vacuum, politics came to be transmuted and was waged around and in the complex bureaucratic procedures of social democracy and corporatism, in the changing definitions of the 'good teacher' driven by circumstance and in the daily aspects of schoolwork. The politics of teaching became waged in a war of position, kept in place by a policing of the boundaries.

Finally, it would be an error to emphasize the politics of work and exclude the way in which teachers used and were used by social movements to extend the definition and nature of teaching, the politics and policies which contained it and the kind of society which contained them.

Notes

1 I am not interested (at least for the purposes of this essay) in the micro-political relations in schools, although the politics of the school labour process, of which micro-politics is a part, is of importance. However, the micro politics of teachers' work and union activity is a new field which appears to reduce politics to a form of interpersonal behaviour for the achievement of private or group aims or for their resistance.

2 This move towards Labour or socialist parties by teachers appears to have been a common phenomenon in the West in the early years of this century, viz., in Canada and France.

3 Examples of the large and small incidents that were used to attack teachers as being 'political' can be found in Lawn (1987a). This is not just an historical phenomenon. Rural areas and small schools in England and Wales are prone to this problem today. The position of a union representative in a school in a rural area is almost saintly. They sacrifice themselves for the sake of others as there is no chance of promotion or an easy life. Whatever they do they are seen by the local managers as intruders on their 'natural relations' with their employees.

4 The idea of the 'good teacher' is a heuristic device only; there is no intention to suggest that there is a preferred version of the teacher. It is a lens to view the employer's or the teacher's version of the teacher in any one period.

2 The Spur and the Bridle: Changing the Mode of Curriculum Control

Professionalism is a highly specific and contextualized idea which is used in contemporary educational writing as a commonsense way of describing or explaining the work of the English teacher. Indeed the teacher and professionalism are so closely bound together in descriptions of work, careers and governance that it seems impolite to raise questions about the meaning of professionalism as to do so risks impugning English teachers. Professionalism is such an affirmative word, with many good associations, that it appears to be beyond critique. Researchers may begin with a short foray into its meanings but then lose their bearings and treat it as a descriptive term in the research. Its very embeddedness in the language of education is remarkable when it is recognized that it is so closely associated with the modernizing tendency in English education and was rooted in a quite specific socio-political and education context. Partly a response to exigency and partly a sophisticated attempt to manage teachers, the language of professionalism, responsibility and autonomy was generated to explain why English teachers were different to those elsewhere and why they didn't need to be involved with the politics of education (and later society). Only in retrospect, from the vantage point of the 1990s where progress in education has been so damaged by spurious reforms and the teachers' professional claims to education dismantled by the sidelining of their associations is it possible to ascertain the shape and purpose of professionalism as a controlling and yet useful myth.

In this chapter the rise of the idea of teacher autonomy in England, a close relation of professionalism for much of the century, is analysed and associated with a particular method of government in education. The foundation of that peculiarly English method of controlling education, through rhetoric and financial and other regulations, was laid in the 1920s and I argue that methods of colonial government were used to control teachers, particularly the idea of indirect rule. The paper will explore this notion through key events in the mid-1920s, centering upon the Board of Education, the President (Lord Eustace Percy) and the Permanent Secretary (Sir L. Selby-Bigge).[1]

In retrospect, teacher autonomy as an exploratory idea in curriculum control in England and Wales may now be seen as historically specific to the period 1925–80. Throughout this period it appears to provide an explanation for events in which teachers are seen as 'professionals' engaged in a 'partnership' with local and central government. In recent years a shift in educational policy and a return to overt, centralized administrative controls in education have muted or replaced this once common explanation in the curriculum field of autonomy, professionalism and partnership. What we lack is a satisfactory account of the events which moved the system of educational government from being centrally controlled to being decentralized or from a period when teachers were seen as municipal servants to one when they were seen as semi-autonomous professionals.

Some account has been given by White (1975) who described how, in the Education Code for 1926, the detailed regulations which had previously governed the curriculum of the elementary school and the training of its teachers were reduced or eliminated. During the course of his essay in explanation of this event, White raised a number of hypotheses: it was a change from statutory to mandatory authority; it was for reasons of finance; it was an attempt to contrive the separation of elementary from secondary education (by not deregulating the latter); it was intended to forestall the changes which would be required by a socialist government. White's own preference is for a hypothesis which sees the Conservative administration apparently trying to separate elementary from secondary educational provision in order to forestall the Labour Party programme of 'Secondary Education for All'. White's essay is a meticulous and reasonable explanation of events and is an attempt to connect historical research, policy study and curriculum control as its main focus in this period.

Brian Simon has also recorded the way in which the President of the Board of Education, Eustace Percy, operated and, in particular, the way in which he had to manage contradictory pressures from the Cabinet (Simon, 1974). The first pressure came from the need to reduce spending on education and this was urged upon Percy by Chamberlain and Churchill. The other came from a desire to create a positive Conservative educational policy which would draw votes back from Labour, a policy which was backed by Conservative Party officials, ex-MPs, and later by Baldwin himself. Simon also richly details the political problems which were created by Percy through his intransigence and inexperience, something which contrasts with the statesmanlike image of his memoirs and which stands as a corrective to the argument which follows.

My own approach to this period of educational change was guided by both White's and Simon's accounts but I had initially come to it by a different route. My previous research (Lawn, 1983) had focused upon the actions of organized teachers in the first two decades of the century. Prominent among its findings was evidence of considerable unrest among teachers, culminating in a series of disputes and strikes and a general movement towards the Labour Party. In response to this unrest, in which the teacher was characterized as 'a social danger', the Lloyd George coalition government through H.A.L. Fisher, the President of the Board of Education, had reorganized the pay structure of the teachers through the Burnham Committee, created a new Education Act and, most of all, offered teachers a vision of their new professional status. By the mid-1920s the teachers were again on the political agenda and the Baldwin Government, through Eustace Percy, became concerned with the question of teacher control and allegiance. It was felt by leading Conservatives that the 'drift of teachers toward the Labour party' (Lawn, 1983, p. 228) could endanger their position as the 'natural' party of government. In this paper I first of all wish to explore the political question of control over teachers and the way in which Eustace Percy saw the problem and tried to deal with it. Secondly, I wish to re-examine White's hypothesis that the regulations controlling the elementary and teacher-training curriculum were dismantled to forestall them being used by a radical Labour Government to alter fundamentally the content and the kind of education given in elementary schools. There is evidence that the dismantling of detailed regulations was not a deregulation of the system but a shift to a different mode of control. This will be discussed using the writings of Selby-Bigge (1927) and Lord Lugard (1923).

The general argument in the paper is that teacher unrest and the need to alter the nature of control in education produced an administrative and political solution which has strong similarities to colonial government by 'indirect rule'. It was not a question of moving from a regulated to a deregulated education system but of moving from a system of direct control to one of indirect control. This solution was intended to enable the Board of Education to continue operating the education system cheaply and efficiently, from its point of view, but with a lighter hand, yet, if necessary, more closely than before.

The Situation in 1926

Eustace Percy was appointed President of the Board of Education by Baldwin in 1924 and held the post for four years. Percy felt himself to be part of a new move in the government of education. After decades of neglect by the Liberal and Tory governments the state interventionist policies of the Lloyd George Government in the First World War had produced a determined President of the Board of Education in H.A.L. Fisher, but this policy appeared to founder in the early 1920s with the return of the older policy of cutting state expenditure, a policy which was consistently followed by Percy's senior Cabinet colleagues Churchill and Chamberlain. Percy, together with Baldwin, the Prime Minister, felt that the Conservative Party was becoming in danger of losing its 'natural right' to govern if it continued in this way. Party managers had warned them about the way in which teachers were moving to Labour, something which had been seen in a series of by-elections and in local elections (viz. a Labour council in Sheffield). After the defeat of 1922 even Baldwin had taken notice of this drift. It was not just the number of teachers voting Labour but the fact that they were seen as good organizers and influential in the local communities which weighed with Party managers. In another way, the worry for the Conservatives was also the question of the social danger presented by teachers; they had earlier been seen in this way by Lloyd George, and talk of subversion and unpatriotic acts by teachers was rife throughout the Party (Lawn, 1983).

What were the teachers doing? Briefly, by 1920 elementary teachers in the NUT had become involved in a salary campaign against their local authorities for a decent salary scale in a period when most of them were on a fixed sum in a period of high inflation. Most of the local associations had been involved in disputes and some in extended strikes. They drew on popular support quite often from working-class parents and were opposed by rate payer candidates such as shopkeepers and industrialists — those who paid the bill. Teachers had increasingly adopted socialist ideas, and the idea of affiliation to the Labour Party, though defeated, had concerned the union for several years. Guild Socialists, the Fabians and the Independent Labour Party all saw a key role for teachers in reconstructing society. The dream of an education service with a full partnership by teachers was expressed in this period as a professional syndicalism-control of a service by its workers.

By 1924, post-war militancy was in retreat, situated in a number of sporadic strikes against local authorities, and professional syndicalism was mainly seen as a vote for Labour. Yet the grievances which had started the teachers' offensive were still in place — their pay award was being threatened by national cuts in spending and by local council resistance. Most of all, their control of their own work was very low. They were at the mercy of heads, governors, vicars and inspectors as well as local councillors. Elementary teachers referred constantly to irksome regulation and petty controls and felt the State did not value their contribution to the education service.

Percy's correspondence with Conservative members of Parliament on the issue of subversive teachers was extensive. They were concerned at the numbers of Labour Party teachers and membership of the Teachers' Labour League, an independent left-wing teachers' group that was to decline in significance after its expulsion from the Labour Party (Lawn, 1985). A popular solution for their apparent loss of political control over the teachers was the idea of the oath of allegiance. Members like Col. Vaughan-Morgan, MP for Fulham East, worried about the effect of left-wing teachers on the 'youth of the country during their most susceptible years', the Conservative Party HQ asked Percy to institute a 'religious loyalty test', and a Society for the Promotion of Duty and Discipline demanded that the oath be made compulsory for all teachers in state-aided schools. A Subversive Teachings Bill was also proposed in order to discipline teachers. The local and national press (such as the *Daily Mail, The Times* and the *Morning Post*) kept up a regular barrage of examples of, and complaints about, 'communistic teaching' and unpatriotic teachers and tried hard to associate Labour Party membership for teachers with subversion of the State.

Percy wrote to Sir Charles Yate a letter explaining his approach to the teacher question. He explained to the MP that the idea of an oath of allegiance, while dramatic, would be ineffective: The subversive propaganda of the present day is concerned with the class war and with attacks on religion. We all know from everyday experience that the holding or propagation of such opinions is generally regarded as quite compatible with professions of loyalty to the King.

If Sir Charles Yate was still not convinced by this argument, and many of Percy's own backbenchers were not, he then added:

> What could be worse from your point of view than to encourage a conception that teachers are servants of a Government in the same way as Civil servants, and therefore must teach in their schools precisely what any future Labour Government may tell them to teach. (Lawn, 1987a, p. 119)

In a sense, Percy was dealing with a moral panic among his party and his class, based on a feeling that insurrection had broken out, led by the teachers. The natural order of things was being threatened or subverted. This was seen whenever teachers stood as Labour candidates, when they canvassed in council by-elections, or when they no longer left the vicar and the farmers in control of parish politics. It was all part of a 'Bolshevization' of teaching and a campaign to 'poison' the youth. The mere fact of Labour Party membership could be seen as subversive to the State in the shires. Percy shared their sense of rising disorder but his strategic sense, his concern for a forward policy in educational administration, led him to a different solution. This solution he offered to Yate:

> I still believe that the best safeguard against such irregularities is to give teachers a sense of reasonable independence and not to subordinate them too much either to a Central or to a Local Authority. (Lawn, op. cit.)

This was Percy's solution — to keep control and yet to manage the teachers more effectively and safeguard the natural, political order of things. This was the approach favoured by a majority in his own party but his means to that end was in opposition to their own. But Percy was not offering deregulation or decentralization; I believe, unlike John White, that Percy intended to establish a strong, strategic and ideological role for the central authority. To establish this view, I wish to discuss Percy's conception of administration, culled from his writings and references, and the view of his Permanent Secretary, Selby-Bigge, derived from his treatise on the work of the Board of Education. Secondly, I want to consider the possible influence of Lugard on Percy and the main features of 'indirect rule' as outlined in Lugard's book and mentioned, if only briefly, by Percy in his memoirs.

Controlling Education

Percy, in his essay on the civil service, began his argument, about the necessity for a new administrative machinery in foreign policy, with a comment on the French Revolution, stating that *no* revolution has ever happened except in a country where the administrative system has broken down . . . If this country today stands in any danger of revolution, it is because its administrative system is becoming too over-burdened and too complicated for efficiency. 'Concentration, specialization, and restriction are the essential of any administrative system' (Percy, 1922, pp. 37–59).

This was not an argument that administrative breakdown caused revolution but that it was a symptom of the breaking-down of policy-making and administration under an accumulation of traditional burdens. Percy argued, in the context of the conduct of the war and the conclusion of peace, for a form of exact administration in departments of state (the civil service) but also for a new 'vitally important sphere of "high policy"'. Percy's examples, drawn from foreign policy, led him to the conclusion that there needed to be a continuity in policy, a logical line of thought encapsulated within it and a concentration of responsibility.

In the years before the events of 1926, Percy can be seen as a theorist of administrative policy, a person who wished to organize a system of administration in such a way that responsibility would be centred on the Secretary of State. The civil service would be organized to carry out instructions clearly and consistently, advising, where necessary, on the possible limitations of policy. Policy creation and expert advice were to reside in the same department.

Percy, on the basis of this article, at least, cannot be seen as a President of the Board of Education who, in releasing direct controls over the service, did so by accident. This action must have made sense to Percy in relation to advice he was receiving from his Board officials, the particular needs of his party at the time and a long-range policy he was developing. Despising improvisation, he was unlikely to offer teachers, his pressing problem, a sop which would only complicate his task later on. What 'high policy' is evident in his action? More clues to this are found in Percy's memoirs.

For him, 'The building up of an effective national system of education by positive administration had never been regarded as a major political interest' (Percy, 1922, p. 93). The exception to this rule was the appointment of H.A.L. Fisher. But in Percy's view the miscalculation in Fisher's overambitious plans — his lack of accurate costing and the consequence of rapid development in education — rendered them susceptible to short-term economies in periods of financial stringency. Percy wrote at some length, in his memoirs, of the rise in demand for 'equality of opportunity' in the country and his colleagues' ignorance of this, of the revolutionary frame of mind present in the country, of a romantic educational philosophy ('school of Dewey') among teachers and of large-scale unemployment and its effects on children. In a real sense Percy set the scene in his memoirs for the necessity of his own statesmanlike intervention. He would be the first real administrator and policy-maker to develop the foundations of a national system of education. Policy-making and administration were, for him part of a wider purpose. To be a statesman, to have vision, to 'form and foster a body of political thought and morals', was vital. It would be his own memorial, perhaps even the 'rallying point of a nation'.

It is worth noting, however, that his own public interventions on teachers in the late 1920s were frequent and fully reported and that they do not create the same impression of a statesmanlike, thoughtful person which he tries so hard to project in his memoirs. Instead, the tone and content are polemical — he talks of 'a danger that threatened education', of 'propaganda' and 'evils of this kind' when referring to members of the Teachers' Labour League. Indeed, as will be seen later, his speeches were intended to placate the Conservative backbenchers and voters, to serve as a warning, to divide the radical teachers from the others and to turn attention away from the high policy he was creating.

The idea of a streamlined administrative system is outlined by Selby-Bigge. He argued, in 1927, that the reason the curriculum regulations, and the other regulations upon the local authorities, were reduced was because of the development and stability of the system. But, in the same chapter, he also said that: 'The Board's regulations were subjected to a process of evaporation which dissipated their more liquid, volatile and aromatic components and left only a residue of financial solids.'

It is the financial solids we can look to — the payment of the grant. No longer bound by detail, the Board now referred to general, not particular, regulations. They were general because the grant was not to be paid at the 'discretion' of the Board, 'throwing more weight' (Selby-Bigge's words) on general terms such as 'recognition, approval, satisfaction, efficiency, sufficiency and suitability'. As he pointed out later, these regulations appear to give a greater freedom to local authorities but are 'more absolute because of a more general discretion to the Central Authority'. The grant was to be paid if the Board, in its discretion, decided what was or was not 'suitable' to be undertaken, and so on. Decentralization was a tactical move, in response to increasing political pressure, made to secure continued strategic control.

To restate their position, there was to be no question of loss of control, only a review about what was the best way to control.[2] Percy argued for a streamlined and specialized administrative system, while Selby-Bigge shows how this could work by substituting particular, for general, rules and regulations.

In his search for a theory of administration Percy used Lugard's 'indirect rule' and in a chapter of his memoirs, called 'Indirect Rule in a Social Service', he discussed the trend after the First World War to a 'method of administration . . . "indirect rule" — a rule as indirect as any that Lugard invented for African territories', and commented later that it 'was even more applicable to teachers than to local authorities' (Percy, 1958, p. 123). The key to the events of 1926 lie in Percy's view of high policy — a theory of administration and control — and it is necessary to reconstruct the Lugard theory of 'indirect rule' to see how it influenced Percy's idea of strategic, covert control.

'Indirect Rule'

What was Lugard's theory of administration, 'indirect rule'? From Lugard's writings and from commentaries upon the practice of colonial administration the following information can be obtained: 'indirect rule' was a means of administering colonies in a way which did not involve direct, centralized administrative control, which was seen as being expensive and, in retrospect, disruptive of the 'natural' social order in the colony. Lugard's book *The Dual Mandate* was the complete handbook upon how this form of administration did work or should work and it became very influential in the training of the governing elite, the Resident and District Officers. It was a peculiarly English method of control and administration very different from the French central-ized model, and open to the charge that it was also a more subtle and hypo-critical form of control, dressed up as the 'fairest' and most suited to local circumstances. Control was exercised through the British Resident and District Officers, who administered the region through local chiefs or their headmen. Advice was offered directly to the local Emir, perhaps, by the Resident; the Emir then instructed the local headmen. In this model, the Emir was the chief ruler and the Resident the counsellor, but the advice offered had to be fol-lowed and the Emir had 'no right to place or power unless he renders his proper services to the State' (Lugard, 1923, p. 203). In theory, chiefs were elected by the traditional system but where they did not exist the British invented them and District Officers could exert pressure in favour of their own candidates. With the Resident's advice came a proportion of the local taxes which the Emir had collected.

The principles underlying this model are as follows. Although power was apparently decentralized or even entirely locally based, there was a strong central coordinating authority. Continuity was obtained by means of official memoranda, published regularly, which were the sources of reference and authority for the Resident. There was uniformity of principle, but the mode of application varied with local traditions and customs. Control has to be exer-cised sensitively without damaging the authority of the local chiefs, yet it had to remain in the hands of the educated class elite. A significant feature of this approach was that, while the day-to-day problems of administration, were delegated to the local area, the central administration retained overall strategic control and could develop mutual understanding, sympathy and cooperation between the government and its people. In a sense, then, central administra-tion retained control and yet appeared not to do so; indeed, it even seemed to mediate in its own conflicts.

There is no direct evidence that Percy had read Lugard's book or that they had met. Percy left no papers and the only reference made to Lugard was the one quoted earlier from his memoirs. Lugard was an important adviser to the Colonial Office at the same time Percy was at the Board of Education but the probability is that Lugard's ideas were becoming generally known in the circles in which Percy moved. It is likely that Percy read *The Dual Mandate* since the parallels and congruencies between the problems of colonial admin-istration and educational administration are clear from the description offered here.

In one very pertinent passage in his memoirs, Percy did acknowledge some dangers of 'indirect rule':

Educational policy might in practice be worked, not by personal touch with a diversity of local authorities [that is, the Lugard model] but by negotiations with a national Association of Education Committees [the chiefs as a body], [or] an even more centralised National Union of Teachers [the natives, organized]. (My interpretation in brackets.)

The danger was that these organized groups could produce the 'dense[st] screen that can shut out Whitehall from real tactical control of a social service' (Percy, 1958). This, of course, is what the system of 'indirect rule' was designed to overcome. But, in practice, it appeared Percy was able to operate by personal touch with local Directors of Education who were unwilling 'to play at caucus politics'. As in colonial Africa, the chiefs were themselves in danger from caucus politics, from independence movements, or, in Percy's world, from the Labour Party and the NUT.

Further parallels between my description of 'indirect rule' and the Percy /Selby-Bigge view of administration can be drawn. The memoranda became the *Handbook of Suggestions for Teachers*, which continued to offer curriculum content and timetable allocations until the 1950s saw it turn into primary education (Gordon, 1988, pp. 41–7). From what little evidence we have about what elementary teachers actually did, the Handbook appears to have ruled their lives and circumscribed their practice. Then there is the question of the officers. Are these the inspectors? If so, Selby-Bigge pointed out in his book that when the regulations become less detailed and more general, the 'satisfaction' of the Board about the working of the system would need to 'be derived more than ever from inspection' (Selby-Bigge, 1927). The Inspector's function in fact altered from being concerned with individual cases (schools) to 'areas' (Rhodes, 1981). Then these are the 'financial solids' mentioned earlier; the Emir gets a share of the local taxes returned to him. This block grant increased local services or the power of the local authority but it also left it at the mercy of a central authority which could withdraw or reduce the grant or change the conditions under which it could be obtained.

Percy's contribution to the administration of education lay, tactically and strategically, in releasing the central authority from direct control of the system. This allowed it to appear as a broker or referee, talking of cooperation and understanding between government and people, which for all intents and purposes meant local authorities and their teachers. Until a local crisis or national emergency appeared, the central authority appeared to be neutral in the system it was controlling (or perhaps, more fairly, trying to control). Percy's high policy saw him offering the teachers, the 'natives', a new model of 'reasonable independence' and professional autonomy and talk of their 'essential soundness'.

Conclusion

Percy needed to solve the political question of the control of the teachers. The teachers were seen as being a force subversive of state authority, drifting towards the Labour Party and even capable of 'poisoning' the country's youth. In essence, teachers were becoming independent and threatening to the natural party of government, the Conservatives. This was Percy's immediate problem, something which continued correspondence with his backbenchers did not allow him to forget. Indeed, he appeared to spend most of 1927 and 1928 making public speeches attacking the left-wing minority of teachers and trying to separate them from the rest by appeals to their reason and soundness. Percy could do this since he had appeared to deregulate and decentralize the government of education. This was the appeal to the teachers' 'sense of reasonable independence' that he tried to convince Sir Charles Yate was so necessary. There was an attempt to seduce the teachers away from their syndicalist programme for self-government and their drift to Labour. Before he could make this appeal he had deregulated the teacher-training and elementary school curriculum and so was removed out of the focus of the teachers' discontent. A close reading of the events of this period and, most of all, of Percy's administrative theory, suggests that the deregulation was a tactical manoeuvre. Percy was convinced of the need for a visionary high policy, one that would concentrate responsibility on the centre and provide a continuity of policy. His model became the Lugard idea of 'indirect rule', a colonial system of apparent decentralization yet with control obtained by a system of grants, of local agents, of official memoranda and close inspection. The events of the mid-1920s moved the system of educational control from that of overt centralized control to that of covert centralized control. The regulations were reduced to general terms ('approval', 'efficiency' etc.), a move which appears to give independence to a local authority in its grant-giving. The Inspectorate were reorganized to assist the Board more efficiently in this new situation. The *Handbook of Suggestions* continued to influence the training and practice of elementary school teachers.

It is ironic that this clear reorganization of the system to increase central control, quite openly discussed by Selby-Bigge and absolutely central to the notion of 'indirect rule', should be seen in retrospect as the key period in the rise of that peculiarity of the English, a system of partnership in education between the centre, the local authority and the teachers. Percy was successful in his high policy in a way he could not have imagined. He released central government from day-to-day control and yet retained good, strategic control. At the same time he was praised for decentralizing the system. For the new role which he created for the President of the Board of Education he provided that of ideologue. New ideas about the soundness of teachers and their essential reasonableness and, no doubt, the important role of local government and of negotiation and consensus, issued forth. The rise of that particular version of professional responsibility and autonomy, as a form of service to the neutral state, can now be seen to be, in part, Percy's creation (Lawn, and Ozga, 1986, pp. 225–38).

Notes

1 It should be seen as both an extension and a qualification of an essay dealing with the same period and having a similar purpose — John White's (1975) 'The end of the compulsory curriculum'.
2 Selby-Bigge and Percy both used horse-riding as a metaphor in explaining their method of control. Selby-Bigge suggested how the whip could be left behind and Percy talked of the balance between using the spur and the bridle. Percy made it plain that the rider chose the path and the pace.

3 Modernizing Professionalism; A Culture of Inquiry and the Teachers' Labour League

The development of modern schooling was not just a series of administrative decisions made nationally and locally nor was it just a series of contingent steps in which crises were avoided and control established. The idea of indirect rule might have shaped a strategy for managing schools and local authorities but it was a necessity created out of the rise of modern schooling, its inadequate structures and cumbersome curriculum controls. Local education authorities operated with local aims, often related to ratepayer power, when national government was increasingly concerned about economic competition, efficiency, controls on the expansion of secondary education and the purposes of elementary education. As part of the reconstruction of controls over the school system, indirect controls operated alongside new shared government bodies, like the Burnham panel advising on teacher salaries across the country. A modern schooling system emerged, moulded by the need to create new forms of sophisticated controls, to manage the direction of a local/national elementary education service and to manufacture a new secure and stable teacher. A powerful discourse of modernization included within it the idea of the professional with defined responsibilities and freedoms. This discourse was partially created by teachers themselves and in reaction to them and their actions. Modernizing education depended upon the creation, control and domestication of teachers. At the same time it gave an opportunity and a language to teachers operating within progressive social movements to develop their own agendas for change. The language of modernizing allowed some teachers to create spaces for change within their own groupings and within their schools.

This essay is an exploration of these teachers and their contemporary interests, following their attempts to organize themselves and develop their own arguments. They had two objectives, clearly seen in retrospect, to survive as a political and organized force in teaching and to develop an authenticity in their theory and practice in teaching. The period in which they operated heightened their responses and sharpened the conflicts with their employers and with their political and union colleagues but it did involve them in international alliances, local class-based campaigns and cross-union lobbying. Their political ideas may appear dated and narrow but they are a product of their time and should not obscure the importance of their action and beliefs. It is part of the argument of the paper that these teachers had an important influence on the shape and content of English education in the post-war period yet that they were themselves drawn into the modernizing project and determined by its concerns.

The modern school was partially created by the actions of progressive actors, including teachers, working in parallel to, alongside and in opposition to the policy makers. The new management of schooling could not manage indirectly the need for some teachers to organize to shape their own view of education and to resist changes they were opposed to. They did not act alone although in retrospect their achievements might not appear great. What is important is that they made a start in challenging the operation and purpose of education by informing themselves of alternative possibilities, in England and in Europe, and by clarifying their arguments. In this chapter, I want to look firstly, at the way these teachers were influenced by a social movement which wrote them into a new role in the reconstruction of society and then secondly, to explore the educational studies of some of the teachers as they sought to develop a coherent view of new educational practice. I am going to use the Teachers' Labour League, a group of teachers, which in their range of labour and socialist opinion, represent in the 1920s a clear example of the new opportunities open to teachers to shape the system of education.[1] Of course, they worked in opposition and against prevailing notions of mass education and the results of their work would only emerge later as they gained influence and the system of education changed in the post-war period. Although small in number, they influenced education at a later time in curriculum practice, against intelligence testing and toward progressive practices in the classroom. Although oppositional, they worked with the grain of educational reconstruction, pushing limited attempts to manage mass education into a wider modernization. Ironically, in so doing they helped to substantiate the myth of professional engagement, a myth that was partially created in order to manage them.

In this chapter, I will outline the rise of a diffuse socialist culture among teachers in England and Wales which grew in scope and influence during and after the First World War. This culture was not homogeneous and even contained elements of socialism that were often mutually hostile, for instance utopian and materialist perspectives, yet, although diffuse, this culture or cultures was perceived as a social danger to the State by old established ruling parties. Socialist cultures waxed and waned in teaching and could act as a magnet for different discontents or as a vehicle for particular progressive policies. Education was at the core of these alliances and sometimes the possibilities of change seemed to attract unlikely partners. The Teachers' Labour League grew within this optimistic social culture and its membership and journal flourished until political divisions made it impossible to continue and the TLL turned into a revolutionary and militant organization and an instrument of Communist Party policy. What is interesting is how this small group of disparate colleagues was seen in the 1920s as a danger to the social order which is probably less to do with their actions or power than their symbolic rejection of the prevailing ruling mores; these would include ideas about the social and political place of the teacher, their natural employers and the creation and continuation of state policy in education. Of course they were just one of several (and much more important) groups of workers who were unionizing, moving to labour or taking direct action in the early 1920s. Nonetheless, it is of interest to explore the views and actions of these teachers in the TLL as they try to create alternative educational ideas and practices. They were the forerunners of traditions of action research in classrooms or critical enquiry in educational practice which are themselves legitimated by later claims to professional responsibility for teachers. In a way the TLL modelled the range of inquiries and activities which later educators would improve under the banner of teacher professionalism.

Socialisms in/around Education

In 'Servants of the State', I described the developing discourse of social and political change, expressed in fictional and polemical essays and novels, which drew upon ideas of educational change as a metaphor for the new changes which would be possible in society under socialism. At the same time teachers were attracted to the Labour Party and to socialist ideas and plans in significant numbers between 1915 and 1925. It was not simply a resentment of Conservative efficiency drives and anti-elementary education ideas which drew to labour but the visions of change. Socialist ideas, from the Fabians to the syndicalists, had percolated discussions among teachers about the new role of elementary education and the elementary teachers in the production of a new society. For many teachers, ideas from the Fabians or guild socialists had been grafted on to their discontents with their local employers and key words like 'professional self-government' began to alter in meaning and consequently in proposed operation as they became suffused with socialist terminology about the State, social responsibility and the nature of work. The influence of socialist writers like Sydney and Beatrice Webb, G.D.H. Cole, H.G. Wells, R.H. Tawney, and significantly in this period, a writer like A.S. Neill (who joined the socialism of the guild socialists to a detailed if idiosyncratic intervention in the New Education discussion) was important to teachers even if it was at second or third hand. Although ideas and programmes differed they jointly offered a new vision of teaching as a major service in the reconstruction of society, the antithesis of the teachers' conditions of work at the time.

The Labour Party programme '*Labour and the New Social Order*' (1918) appealed to all the community to involve themselves in the creation of a new social order by the application of science and rationality to the running of every branch of society, by planned cooperation and the 'widest possible participation in power' (Williams, 1947). It argued for a legal basic wage and a system of public work programmes, including schools. In other words, for teachers, it was matching their financial problems with solutions, their educational poverty with expansion and their lack of power and control in their 'industry' by participation and public ownership. There was a feeling of real change and this was a source of attraction for teachers. The effect of the Labour Party policies and progressive writers claiming a central place for teachers in a new society must have been intoxicating for some teachers treated like servants by the Church, local business councillors and the school inspectors alike or those in touch, through family or friends or the media, with a diversity of public discussion in the cities.

For example, popular books like H.G. Wells' *New Worlds For Old* appealed to teachers directly. For Wells, socialism was a moral and intellectual process and he placed teachers at the heart of this process as agents of a process of national cultural renewal. He offered a radical new outlook on the teaching process under socialism — new and improved schools, better salaries and pensions and newly responsive children. He offered a renewed vocation for the public good, an irresistible vision for teachers. When the appeal was most effective it 'worked with the grain' of teacher aspirations, combining a powerful social role with improved conditions of work.

Broader movements, like Guild Socialism, with their own journals, denounced a system which saw workers as no more than 'living' tools in the production process, deserving no consideration or freedom. Work being central to life, the workers could never be fully satisfied nor able to fully serve the community until they controlled the means of production — in the workplace by self-government. This self-government would operate through guilds, based on trade unions, and it was this idea which appealed to some teachers, because of its compatibility to older ideas of professional self-government. G.D.H. Cole, in 1920, talks of its appeal to professional workers, such as teachers because it had concentrated its work entirely upon the question of industrial and professional self government.

Cole himself argued that:

> The internal management and control of each industry or service must be placed, as a trust on behalf of the community, in the hands of the worker engaged in it; but he holds no less strongly that full provision must be made for the representation and safeguarding of the consumer's point of view. (Cole, 1920b)

Again, socialism was equated with self-government and with control over work. Later in the book, the equation is made directly between teachers and their administration of the education system, subject, of course, to the 'ownership' of education, on behalf of the consumers, parents and children, by the State. An entire chapter in *Guild Socialism Restated* (Cole, 1920b) was given over to an analysis of how this professional control would work in education. This could be a highly democratic education guild, capable of allowing schools to organize their own educational direction. Here teachers would not have *the* central place in societal renewal but instead were seen as part of that new category, 'the professional or brain worker'. 'Working with the grain' was Cole's view but perhaps teachers saw in these proposals a way of democratizing their industry and freeing themselves from the petty restrictions of their work. A.S. Neill was perhaps the best propagandist for an education guild; at this time he was a schoolteacher in a Scottish council school. Throughout his first book *A Dominie's Log*, Neill illustrates the difficulties of the progressive class teacher. The popularity of this book was partly due to his audacity in criticizing his employers, something which many rural teachers could not afford to do, and partly to the sense of educational change he conveyed. Neill expressed clearly the mixture of socialism, trade unionism, humanistic educational enterprise and professional control which weaves in and out of these arguments among teachers. It is through the popular writings of people like Cole, Wells and Neill that discontent could form itself into new possibilities: new ways of seeing their problems, new allies to help them change, new languages of critique and new actions.

Changing Teachers, Changing Schools

The main focus for some of these teachers in the early 1920s was the Teachers' Labour League. The League in its short history reveals the problems that a variety of radical teachers had in coping with each other and developing common strategies at a time when there was severe unemployment and they themselves could be summarily sacked for being 'left-wing'. The League was never really influential among teachers though it was, without any doubt, seen as extremely threatening by the Conservative governments of the 1920s. It comprised at its peak about 800 teachers but in the main was about 600. The League was formed in 1923 but its roots lay in teacher militancy in 1917, it was concentrated around London but had branches dotted around England. In its early years, it received active support from newly appointed professors of education, like J.S. Findlay, from some trade unions, from A.S. Neill, from prominent Labour Party figures and from workers' education bodies (such as the Plebs League). It acted as an advisory body to the Labour Party, discussing its education policy at conferences and publishing articles by Neill and others on what should be happening in education. By 1925 it was divorced from the Labour Party, caught up in international divisions in the left: its broad church approach was soon replaced by an increasing dogmatism about teachers and the working class and the Labour Party constructed an advisory group in education from its ex-members. Although it contained within it a non-sectarian spirit there was a syndicalist and militant unionist tendency in the TLL alongside its various radical influences. The syndicalist argument was more straightforward and, for some teachers, more powerful. The means to achieve a proper salary and an end to the petty tyrannies of the workplace was unionization; the strike weapon was fashioned in a period, before and during the war, when half the local associations were in dispute with their employers even though only a handful threatened to strike or did strike. The educational message contained within this movement was about freedom and power; education's major problem was the policies of the ruling class and if this was solved then a new kind of education could emerge.[2]

What of the policies and statements which interested League members? *The Educational Worker*, the League's journal, attacked the celebrations of Empire Day, which often involved the encouragement of jingoism in schools, the bias in history teaching and the right-wing attitudes of the Boy Scouts. Articles argued for the development of nursery education (by Margaret Macmillan), for the values of a new school curriculum and for the new direction on Soviet education. A.S. Neill wrote articles for young teachers. A major part of League policy was the question of full political and civil liberties for teachers, as some teachers, and it only needed the well-publicized few, were sacked from teaching or had to defend themselves strenuously to prevent their dismissal in the aftermath of the failed General Strike of 1926. Consistently the League argued for civil rights for teachers and against the surveillance, informal and formal, of radical teachers. Other parts of the League programme, as expressed in the *Educational Worker*, were equal pay for men and women, the rights of married women to continued employment, teacher and parent representatives on school management committees and against the compulsory out of school activities which were especially common in church schools.

The *Educational Worker* is a useful source for gauging the interests of the League. It attempted to be inspirational and informative from its early days, but not until the late 1920s could it be seen as having a particular line. For example, James Maxton, writing an article on 'The Teacher and Politics', argued for 'high ideals of social life' for teachers, but Dan Griffiths, a Welsh teacher, taking the same subject included salaries, class size, local and national expenditure on education and so forth, in the necessity for teacher involvement in politics. Other elements of its education policy were listed in 1927 (*EW*, vol. 1, no. 8, 1927); teachers should have full political and civil liberties and receive a university education or equivalent. Married women teachers should not be liable to dismissal and there should be equal rates of pay between certificated and experienced uncertificated teachers. On the administration of schools, the League wanted teacher and parent representatives on school management and local education committees. It reported on other areas of its interest such as secular education, parents' councils, central schools, the scout movement and compulsory attendance in schools. A further programme in September 1927 attacked the old grievances of demands upon teachers for compulsory out of school activities, dismissal for political expression or offences and preferential employment for acceptable religious and political views. The League was concerned at the continuing sweated labour of uncertificated and supplementary teachers (*EW*, vol. 2, no. 18, 1928) and a new class of teachers, the commercial teachers (working in private schools and commercial colleges). It urged action on unemployed teachers (*EW*, vol. 1, no. 10, 1927) and on unemployed ex-service teachers, seeing both (with good reason) as a labour reserve used by local education authorities to reduce wages. This was the case at Lowestoft, in Norfolk, where a year-long strike of teachers for the national wage-scales had to overcome the importing of unemployed teachers to run the schools. The Lowestoft strike was of interest in another way. Lowestoft teachers set up their own schools to attract pupils from the struggling council schools. These schools, called welfare centres, had another purpose; a different kind of education emerged in the centres. It did not involve corporal punishment, a major feature of elementary schools at the time. There was a freedom and a cama-raderie between teachers and pupils and the 'children became mentally more alive; they showed a greater capacity for tackling jobs on their own initiative' (*EW*, vol. 2, no. 19). The curriculum consisted of the reading, writing, arith-metic, history, geography, games and used educational films. The key differ-ence in the school appears to have been the solidarity felt by the pupils with the teachers; their parents had sought out the centres to send their children to in support of the striking teachers.

An inspirational example of politics in school was, of course, the Burston Strike School. The struggle by the Burston community and its teachers, Anne and Tom Higdon, in Norfolk which had been going on for several years, had resulted in a new school, the Burston School, established with the aid of voluntary contributions from all over the country. Tom Higdon was on the League's Executive in 1927 (voted in after the split) and spoke at branch meetings on the Strike School and its curriculum. Until League members became familiar with Soviet education after the League organized a touring exhibition in 1931, the Burston school epitomized the socialist changes they expected in the schools. An article about the school, written in December, 1926 (vol. 1, no. 2) probably by C.G.T. Giles told of the 'comradeship', 'self-organization' and 'initiative' at the school. There must have been a general awareness in the League of the kind of socialist curriculum operating at Burston. It included visits to local strikers, collections for Russian famine victims, pro-test meetings about the Sacco and Vanzetti trial, Christian Socialist instruction (Jesus and the poor etc.), visits to union branch meetings and a regular so-cial evening with parents (with cooking by the pupils) (Edwards, 1974, p. 153). At the 1926 Conference Tom Higdon moved a resolution asking branches to investigate the problem of class conscious versus neutral education, using Burston childrens' compositions as examples. In December 1927, the results of the investigation were published. League teachers opposed Empire Day cele-brations, class distinctions in schooling and bias in textbooks but the research showed that although League members were agreed that education in Britain was an instrument of class domination, a smaller number of them felt that the future basis for a state education system should be a class not a neutral ethic. Others felt that a teacher should be free to present all sides of a problem. In other words, the League was aware of what it was against but still working out the basis for what it was for in changing schools.

Groups of League teachers visited Neill's Summerhill School at Leiston, Dora and Bertrand Russell's School and Bedales School in Hampshire. Accounts of their visits describe the schools but also explore their reactions; their interest lay in trying to borrow from these experimental schools a new practice which could be transported into state schools. For example, the London Committee made two visits to Bedales and discussed their visits back in their London meetings; elementary and secondary, art and infants, head and assistant teachers made up the visit. They had disagreed about the Russell's school but Bedales impressed them with its resources, the efficiency of the head, the junior school Montessori practice and the co-education policy. They were concerned that the disciplinary system, although a success, was not democratic as the head appointed the prefects. They were disappointed by the lack of freedom and flexibility in the curriculum in spite of the fact that there were over forty teachers to only 270 pupils. '(The visit) showed us the possibilities of the boarding school and the practicality of coeducation as well as the impossibility of escape under the present system from the deadening grip of examinations' (*EW*, August, 1929).

Although these study trips were important, they began to be over-shadowed by the influence of the Soviet Union and its educational system in the TLL. By the late 1920s searching for experimental education had been replaced by talks about Russian schools by members who had visited the country and the *Educational Worker* produced articles on 'New Theories in Mass Schools' or 'The Five Year Plan in Soviet Schools'.

In 1928, the Education subcommittee of the TLL appealed to members, within an article titled 'Psychological Investigation' to help them study the new psychology and the way it affected schools through the use of intelligence testing. It was the practical result on workers' children of testing that interested them and the League teachers searched for allies in an inquiry in to testing.

So, the interests of the League gradually began to focus down in the 1920s, probably under the influence of the Communist Party members. Visionary appeals and moral disciplining were left behind and a psychology of learning and programmatic union objectives replaced them. The home grown heroism of the Higdons, faced with a local injustice, was replaced by a pre-occupation with Soviet Russia and its new theories of education. Gradually, the League lost touch with many teachers as the decade wore on, it began to distrust teachers in inverse proportion to the trust it placed in the working class. But what the League did was to encourage teachers to question the system under which they worked, to devise new plans for it and to establish the idea that teachers had a role to play in the policies and operation of schooling.

Conclusion

Socialist cultures in teaching developed from the political and social changes taking place in the wider labour movement, and from appeals, programmes and courses of action addressed to or involving teachers. They developed at local level in union alliances or municipal politics, and they were exercised in national debates about the union, the State and the education service. They existed within a period when teachers were on low, fixed incomes, when inflation was growing and when teachers worked in a rudimentary and poorly resourced local system of education in which they had begun to openly dispute with or even strike against management control and their ratepayer employers. The incompatibility of the different versions of workers' control and the means of achieving them may not have been as important to teachers as the way in which workers' control corresponded to and yet revised older teaching cultures associated with professional or craft approaches to control in education. The socialist cultures of work were directed outward into local and national politics and were a reflection of national left policies of different kinds, indeed teachers or ex-teachers were key players in creating those policies in the first place. The creation of a modern, progressive state with a corresponding system of education dominated discussions about education, moving other kinds of visionary ideas about personal morality or social ideals to one side. A few teachers began more focused discussions and educational visits which were aimed at the creation of new school practices. They claimed a right to professional engagement with educational psychology, progressive pedagogies and values education.

These various progressive cultures in teaching may have merged over time in the period of post-war reconstruction and expansion. The modernization and reconstruction project involved direct campaigns and also less direct pressures within the unions and the Labour Party. Distinctions between socialism and educational innovation became less obvious, and could merge in demands for the common school or an advocacy of change in elementary schooling, in the provision of nursery education or through the introduction of an effective social curriculum. They were later associated with union campaigns for unity, for progressive child-centred education, and with Labour Party education programmes. After the Second World War they re-emerged shorn of their revolutionary wing and radical pedagogy, and worked within and even dominated the educational language of professional partnership and consensus. The social danger was partly defused, or more perhaps obviously diffused into a more radicalized professionalism which campaigned for structural changes to the school system and worked within practice and research, as well as in policy platforms, for a common school and an enhanced curriculum.

The League was a vanguard and although its analyses and campaigns were articulate they were ineffectual if they are to be judged by the standards of a mass movement or an elite pressure group. They were squeezed by splits inside the left, wasted effort on internal struggles and were constantly policed by the mass media and local politicians. As a home for members of the Communist Party, it was often attacked in the conservative press in the 1920s and 1930s (and without the League this would continue in the 1950s and 1960s). There was a danger to many teachers if they were seen as being known associates of Communist Party members and joined the League. However, the greatest danger to the vanguard turned out to be the gradually rising living standard of teachers in these decades. Though never generous, for most there was financial security. Other writers have described certain features of the lower middle classes between the wars which may help in understanding the decline of socialist cultures. The lower middle classes were divided, they argue by hierarchies and grades, by small privileges and distinctions of dress, by a system of slow progress up a ladder of incremental work privileges, steadily excluding those below. They were further divided by age and seniority and by gender (the marriage bar and unequal pay). In this light, their altruistic notions of service and welfare could only be based on social superiority in a time of social stasis as the 1930s were. They weren't threatened economically or socially or politically by the manual and skilled working class and no longer searched for alliances with them, forged in local campaigns. Instead the Labour Party could be turned into an instrument for their own purposes and their support for modernization of state provision served teachers' interests and created a sort of alliance with the working class but one distinguished by its unequal nature, so teachers were to be seen as experts and had a special 'service' mission (Samuels, 1983).

A more optimistic view of the League suggests that its legacy lived on within cultures of teaching as a discourse of a modernized professionalism, living within the contradiction of working in the State and yet in opposition to it. The current idea of teachers as active and reflective professionals, inquiring into the intentions and operations of education for the purpose of developing a professional vernacular and practice, as well as campaign material and alliances, is influenced by the activities of the League. They weren't the only ones concerned with educational advance but they claimed a social and political project as teachers and a right to engage with educational practice as teachers. They established the rights of teachers to engage with the purposes and practices of education and so were the forerunners of later groups of teachers engaged in social and educational change. In some ways, they modelled a way of working together as teachers in a political and educational project which was important as an exemplar and as a post-war network for change.

Notes

1 Another group of teachers who began to shape a new system by their developing practice were the feminist teachers of the National Union of Women Teachers, formed in the Twenties. My argument about indirect control, educational change and social danger is based on the TLL. Parts of the argument about educational change and the development of a new practice, in this case through a new feminist culture of work and opposition to developing national policies, applies to the NUWT as well as the TLL.

2 The birthplace of syndicalism among teachers was the Rhondda valley in South Wales, a long, narrow valley, dominated in 1919 by a massive coal industry. The

valley, in common with the other South Wales valleys, had several regular classes on economic theory and industrial history, organized through the Plebs League. Two of the volunteer tutors were also teachers and came to lead the Rhondda teachers' strike, they were W.G. Cove and Gwen Ray. The Rhondda teachers were affiliated to their local Trades and Labour Council and victimization of Cove for being a socialist was only forestalled by the implied threat of the local miners' lodges to strike in his support.

4   The British Way and Purpose: The Spirit of the Age in Curriculum History

In this essay, I attempt to capture some elements of an important period in modern curriculum history, to try to untangle myths and realities and to raise questions, if only in passing, about the influence of Army education on the post-war education system. This essay relies on perceptions and images to untangle the way in which a new form of pedagogy may have been created within a massive adult education programme in the 1940s and in myth and reality is associated with the post-war project to change society and its schools.

A half-remembered myth of the end of the Second World War and the election of the Labour Government in the UK with which I began this research suggests that it was the overseas Army vote that was cohesive in the election and that it was Army education that was so influential on the men and women of the forces in producing that vote. While reading Angus Calder's book *The People's War* two stories immediately served to reinforce this idea, both of them speaking about the radicalizing effect of Army education but from two slightly different angles. One story is of an officer sheltering in a barn while under mortar attack, and finding a corporal and twelve men earnestly discussing 'What shall we do with the Germans after the war?' Another story concerns a very influential wartime Conservative minister, Lord Woolton, talking about Army education as a left-wing plot, something he only began to realize after the election (Calder, 1982, p. 290). Calder's stories raise two images, that of the earnest discussion group and that of a left-wing education coup. It is this contradiction, or tension, between images that will persist within this exploration in curriculum.

I continued to read and research intermittently, collecting odd references to Army education until the time when I began actively to search them out. A secondhand copy of a bound edition of a major textbook, produced as pamphlets, called *The British Way and Purpose*, was my first solid piece of evidence about the intentions of the Army staff within education. The section on education was co-written by Toby Weaver, who later became a deputy secretary in the Department of Education and Science (DES). Peter Woods (1984) inadvertently introduced me to another reference when I read about 'Tom' in his study of a retired teacher and the way in which Tom's 'curriculum' was an expression of his self, especially that created in early life. 'Tom' ran the local section of the Army Bureau of Current Affairs, a major plank of the Army education programme. Next, while working in the Mass Observation archive at the University of Sussex, collecting wartime teacher diaries, I came across a diary that had many references to the way a current affairs class worked as the diarist was its tutor. My initial resistance to the idea that Army education could be a significant force in the social history of education became altered by these references to the shared personnel of Army and civilian life, by the effect it could have on individuals and the way they saw themselves, and by reading about a real class, the teacher pedagogy and the process of its deliberations and arguments. So, finally, I tried to immerse myself in the film and book archives of the National War Museum and developed some 'feel' for the way the idea of current affairs education was organized, in the Army.

In itself the idea of compulsory current affairs discussions conducted by a probably untrained regimental officer, with a handbook of procedures and suggestions at hand, may not appear to be the ideal material to argue for the production of radical social change. The answer, even in an exploration, began to form around purpose, that is the intentions of those creating the programme and those using it, and around context, that is the political and social condition (including battle zones) in which it developed. The same project in a contemporary western professional army could not replicate the particular conditions existing in the citizen armies, particularly the Eighth Army of Italy and the Western Desert, fighting to end the war abroad and build the peace at home. The sources used within this essay fragment into a number of different perspectives: official histories written in the early post-war period dwelling on the organizational structure of the project; handbooks, pamphlets and films used within the discussions and produced at the time in England; personal accounts of involvement, however fleeting; and recent revisionist histories which place Army education as one agency within a period of radical reconstruction or dissent. It is the images of the programme — a tutorial or a Model Army class — current at the time in personal and official statements, and reviewed again in revisionist critique, which it is necessary to study first. It is these images culled from handbooks, pamphlets, and most of all from films, which explain and obfuscate the meaning of Army education. It is not possible to view ABCA films (the Army Bureau of Current Affairs is a part of Army education) on town planning or the importance of the citizen in rebuilding society without recognizing their ideological power. These are not documentary films even though they owe a great deal to the style and direction of documentaries at the time. They are powerful propaganda films directed to the serving soldier, at home or abroad, and calling for them to rebuild the UK. The dark images of the past of poor housing and dirty factories, are replaced by light — a new modern society created by a demobbed citizen's army. They are powerful but indistinct. Beyond these images is a process of education, in makeshift accommodation and with rudimentary equipment, which could take a specific identity, different from its neighbour, making a general call to an optimistic future.

In his book on Army education, Colonel A.C.T. White has a page with two

illustrations on it, one painted, one photographed. The top picture, the painting, is entitled 'Current Affairs' at Balliol 1944 and shows a number of men and
women in uniform, in conversation, either sitting down or strolling around the
grounds of Balliol College, Oxford. The lower picture, called 'Current Affairs'
in Italy 1944, is of a group of about twenty-five soldiers, sitting or standing in
a semi-circle and facing a soldier with arms folded, who is talking. The link
between the two is in their titles 'Current Affairs'; in many other respects they
might appear dissimilar. The intention of the juxtaposition appears to be that
the reader 'sees' the two illustrations as examples of one case. A.D. Lindsay,
the Master of Balliol College described the soldiers of the ABCA classes as
wanting 'to argue and discuss, and they were being encouraged to do so.
There was almost universal testimony that discussion was free, and felt to be
free, that men, non-commissioned officers and officers, discussed together'
(Hawkins and Brimble, 1947, p. 118). (Lindsay himself wrote some of the
discussion pamphlets for the Army's sister programme, The British Way and
Purpose.) This, then, is the connection: both groups are involved in a free
discussion, overriding problems of rank or class or expertise. But while the
quality of the discussion and the soldiers' involvement in it was remarked
upon at the time, there are significant differences between the two illustrations and the worlds they represent.

It was a not uncommon idea at the time that adult education or workers'
education should be seen as an extension of university education. The university extension classes or the Workers' Educational Association both used
images in which the ideas of liberal education were distributed by a university tutor in modest, off campus rooms in chapels or institutes. Even in 1963,
Colonel White felt that the juxtaposition of these two images, the quad and
the field, revealed the real purpose of Army education and, in evaluation,
its success. There is also a tension between these two illustrations which is
revealed by comments or by alternative images and which is embedded in
this essay of reconstruction. The image of the New Model Army, current then
and later, does not fit the travelling Balliol extension class version of education. It could as easily be claimed by ex-members of the Plebs League ('for an
independent Marxist education') or Left Book Club members as their version,
their symbol, created within Army education whatever the intentions of its
organizers:

> I get the impression that there had not been an army in England
> which discussed like this one since that famous Puritan Army which
> produced the Putney Debates and laid the foundations of modern
> democracy. (Hawkins and Brimble, 1947, p. 118)

In a later reference to the New Model Army of the seventeenth century, parallels were drawn with the Levellers (of the Putney Debates) again:

> Cromwell's army . . . spent a considerable part of its time in discussing
> topics very similar to those that were being considered with such

> vigour in the Second World War. In the Leveller's 'Petition to the House of Commons' of September 11, 1648, for example, pleas were made for dealing with such topics as conscription, monopolies, taxes, social security, war criminals and army pay. (Hawkins and Brimble, 1947, p. 158)

This theme of a citizens' army, a New Model Army, discussing the war and post-war reconstruction occurs often in contemporary accounts. A recent history of Communist Party members in the armed forces makes the same reference:

> for the first time since the Parliamentary Army of 1646, troops in the field, and in the rear were openly talking about politics, what the war was about, and what they wanted to come out of the seeds of the post-war Welfare State were sown by Sergeants, Corporals and other ranks. (Kisch, 1985, cover)

They were, in the original sense, agitators, representatives of the lower ranks.

When the Ministry of Information, with the War Office, produced a short film to explain ABCA to troops, in 1943, it began:

> Three hundred years ago an Englishman, Oliver Cromwell, said these words: 'The Citizen soldier must know what he is fighting for and love what he knows.' In that spirit Cromwell created a new Army of the finest fighting men England had to that day known. We've done it again, Britain has made a New Army. (ABCA, 1943)

It continues making the point that training was not just a question of technical military skill and weaponry use but 'like the old Ironsides he [the soldier] takes something more — a weapon of the mind'. This training, and knowing and loving what you are fighting for, was the responsibility of ABCA, and the film explains briefly why it was necessary and how it should work. ABCA discussions were not just about the geography and strategies of the war but about why it was necessary to fight it and continue that fight into peacetime, about having a 'positive belief', a 'weapon of truth and understanding'.

The two images of the wartime education programme, then, are (a) that it was a form of university extension class, a chance to learn and discuss just as the Balliol undergraduates did, or (b) that it was like the New Model Army, winning the war through continuous discussion about strategies and post-war change.

Neither image is without its flaws. It is possible that the apparent discordance between them may be due to slightly different aspects of the forces' education being emphasized. For instance, there had been a regular arrangement for university and Workers' Educational Association lecturers to give 'expert' talks to the troops, usually on Britain (ABCA came later and from within the army not from the adult education committees), but these were 'talks' not current affairs discussions. In a handbook produced to guide officers in the conduct of discussions, by ABCA, a distinction is made between the two.

Lindsay introduced the Model Army idea in concluding his article in the handbook with a parallel between ABCA discussions and the arguments of the earlier citizens' army:

> Lectures, by experts, are no doubt, stimulating and informative and may be more skilful efforts than those of the ordinary regimental officer. They can supplement but do not take the place of informal talks and discussions on a platoon base. Such lectures do not give the same opportunity for the two-way traffic of discussion. Men will ask questions and take part in the proceedings more freely when the audience is small and consists only of fellows in their own platoon then when they are part of a large audience. (ABCA, 1942, p. 11)

This distinction is pointed up within the film when a monologue on town planning by the officer ('An increasing process of suburbanization takes place, all at the behest of industry, which demands a concentration of workers near the factories . . . Now, if we agree to plan we must plan functionally' (ABCA, 1945b, p. 4) is criticized as it 'gives men an inferiority complex'.

So it appears that Army discussions were meant to be like the informal university discussions that took place in Oxbridge, where talking about current affairs was part of the life of the students, something that was reflected in the biographies of the initiators of this idea. The New Model Army is the other image. Again, this is a flawed parallel. The idea of the Cromwellian army came sometime after the war's beginning; Lindsay was writing in late 1941 and the Army ABCA handbook of August 1942 uses the same quotation from Cromwell as the later ABCA film. The idea of the 'soldier-citizen' was used in the first of the British Way and Purpose bulletins, each of which aimed to provide information about the social and political structure of Britain. But while the Cromwellian army of the soldier-citizen was certainly created from above, the discussions remarked upon, such as that of the Levellers, took place in spite of the generals! Talk of Agitators and Levellers aside, the use of the image of the Cromwellian army is related to the necessity of involving the soldiers in thinking about what they were fighting for, not just who they were fighting against. There is also the sense of a democratic army in formation — at least Lord Gorrell remarked upon '[the] new spirit abroad, that spirit of a man being a man "for a' that", which has, in some of its manifestations, at any rate, been decidedly lacking in the past' (Hawkins and Brimble, 1947, p. 159). And to a degree, the handbook talked of a new equality in the army: 'the British Army dares to be democratic because we know that it is through being citizens of a democratic country that we shall win' (ABCA, 1942, p. 9). It was only, of course, to a degree because there was no question of a relaxing of Army discipline and of the direction of the company commander.

The Education Programme

What was the practice that lay beneath these conflicting images? Neither an alfresco Balliol nor the Putney Debates quite fit an early description of the ABCA classes. What was intended to happen is conveyed in the ABCA training film. An early sequence of the film is based in a dug-out soon after the retreat from France; the soldiers were described as having been through a 'mental blitz' for which they had not been prepared. Their conversations are based on exchanging rumours about the war and about secret weapons. The commentary points out that it was not just a question of training physically; soldiers had to be trained in mind as well. A new purpose had to be fashioned to replace rumour.

The handbook describes the purpose of ABCA as in opposition to the 'widespread ignorance' about current affairs in the armed forces and the necessity to raise morale. The two are linked: 'morale is fundamentally a matter of self-discipline and that true discipline is a matter of understanding. The officer seeks, therefore, to cultivate discipline by expanding wherever possible the meaning of an order' (ABCA, 1942, p. 5). The problem of ignorance and low morale was a post-Dunkirk problem and continued until the end of the reverses in the Middle East. In the Army Command's eyes, they eroded the discipline of the forces — without good morale there could not be good discipline. Morale, the handbook continued, develops 'inside you', it is the fusion of a 'group feeling and a personal feeling':

> As to the first, it depends upon everyone in the group . . . feeling the same, feeling confidence in and a sense of comradeship with every other member of the group, from the leader downwards . . . as to the personal elements this arises from a man feeling he has something bigger than himself to fight for . . . a man must have something to fight for which he is prepared to die for. (ABCA, 1942, p. 8)

The purpose of the discussion was to build good morale by allowing an individual to talk on equal terms with others in the group, developing a sense of unity with them and debating differences openly. The group would discuss bulletins, alternately either Current Affairs or War; the former provided a background knowledge of current events, the latter provided military intelligence about the various theatres of war. Later on, further time was set aside to discuss the pamphlets of The British Way and Purpose, dealing with the responsibilities of citizenship and the policies of reconstruction — examples included Local Government, The Responsible Citizen, Working for a Living, Education and the Citizen and Freedom From Fear.

The key to the quality of the discussion, the handbook stressed, lay in the quality of the officer conducting it. Most of the handbook's contents were concerned with the working of the discussion group and the responsibility of the officer for its success. Advice was offered about how to deal with controversy, coaxing the reluctant soldier, preparing questions, working with other officers, supplementing group discussions, and so on. It also offered some criticism of the officer's monologue, as we have seen, and how to overcome a lack of self-confidence. The handbook was a form of distance training. It tried to meet the rising criticism of this ambitious project, particularly that aimed at the cognitive and pedagogical skills of the officers.

The ABCA film had a sequence taken within a sleeping-hut, which, presumably, was to be taken as an example of a group struggling to discuss. The officer begins:

> Well now, I expect you are wondering what this is all about. We're starting something called ABCA. We're going to have an hour's discussion every week of current affairs: and it's going to come out of working time. But it's not going to be just a rest. Now, the idea's this: we're going to have a different subject every week. I'll tell you something about it, and then you'll give your ideas. Get this you're going to do the talking, not me. (ABCA, 1943)

Jenkins, the officer, then introduces the subject of desert fighting, referring to a battle near Tobruk (in Libya), and asks why the armed forces are fighting there. It develops as a question-and-answer session, then where an open question leads to several responses all at once, he chooses a soldier to answer more fully, and another as well [Oh, all right, Hawkins]. This soldier he cuts off in midstream with 'OK, you'll have another chance later' and 'I see you've all got the idea'. It is presumably an example of good practice, controlling but not dominating, and so on. Although they are not underlined in the film, elements of the discussion — on questioning, chairing a session, coping with a garrulous soldier and coaxing a reluctant one — relate to the training handbook. Both the film and the handbook offer a number of means of supplementing the discussions and so improving them: photo-displays, a wall newspaper, quizzes, brainteasers, maps and informational films. ABCA itself produced information films for the armed forces relating to the British Way and Purpose issues. One, Public Opinion, was about freedom of speech and organizing opinions (for example, in the trade unions); another, Town and Country Planning, was about post-war rebuilding, the elimination of homelessness, the preservation of the countryside, and the collaboration of planners and central and local government within a prosperous Britain. A final discussion on the USSR in the training film is worth recording as it represents an approved level of interaction in the discussion:

> **Officer** Now, I want you to ask yourselves, how was it that a nation which only twenty-five years ago went through all the horrors of civil war and revolution, with famine, plague and the complete destruction of its industry, was able to build up an army powerful enough to stand up to and lick the Germans?

Sergeant I think it's (because) they feel they own their own country.
Corporal You just can't beat that sort of people.
Bradley That's all right for them; what about us, though? We don't own our country.
Robertson Don't talk such a lot of rot!
Officer Why do you think that's rot, Robertson?
Robertson It is our country. And if there is an injustice, inequality, it's our fault for allowing it.

A fairly open, if leading, question is offered by the officer; it then moves quickly into a discussion between the soldiers, with an intervention by the officer to allow a further explanation from one soldier. For ABCA, this discussion works — there is equality between ranks, an openness in the topic and the responses, a key facilitating role played by the officer, a relationship made between current affairs and the responsibility of citizenship.

It is necessary to place this discussion within a context which is not just pedagogical but related to purpose. These soldiers are openly discussing another society, comparing it with their own and making a judgment about how to make changes. Implicit in the dialogue is a recognition that another country has somehow successfully fought injustice and inequality, and that a responsibility now lay on the soldiers to do likewise. This is Cromwell's army, then, in the making.

Unity of purpose is forged in the discussion group, a democratic process for a democratic purpose, a weapon against the Nazis but increasingly for the peace:

> When the war is won; when the soldier has once again become a citizen, it is the tool with which he will build the peace. For that is his next job, and it may in the end prove a tougher one than winning the war . . . [ABCA] is also laying the foundations of an enlightened society which will one day enjoy the peace. (ABCA, 1945a, p. 7)

The discussion group, a pedagogical device, was now linked to the social reconstruction of society and described as central to a renewed democratic purpose in that society. The lesson was that commitment to a society was essential to overcome inequalities and to win the war, and that commitment could be created and sustained.

A detailed account of the way in which an Army unit received its first talk, 'War in the Desert', was written by a soldier at the time. This unit's experience was not uncommon, especially in the early days, and it illustrates the difficulties that even a precise and detailed handbook of suggestions has to overcome when an innovation is taking place, more or less simultaneously, across a large number of sites, with unskilled tutors and recalcitrant soldiers.

The education officer was newly appointed and, because of the large number of soldiers in the unit, it was intended that he gave his 'talk' at three different times. Following the instructions of the handbook the officer said: 'It is the wish of the Colonel that these talks should be as informal as possible. He wants you to enjoy them and it is his wish that you may smoke' (Novy, 1985, p. 122). This attempt at informality, the observer reports, was somewhat resented by the men. The tone of the lecture appears to have been like a university lecture — the observer talks of the officer's 'varsity' accent and, as he was a medical officer, complains that it sounded like a lecture to a 'medical students' class. The topic, the first unit in the series on 'War', was about Wavell's desert campaign; yet it was received by them at a time when the campaign had suffered reverses and when the battle for Leningrad was on their minds. Finally, the observer commented:

> It was just a poor rehash óf a poor text. Knowing nothing about tactics he could not illustrate. He had a keen sense that the illustrations given in the text were worn and would only seem stupid to the men. Therefore he talked about the little incidents he remembered in the last war . . . there was a complete absence of questions and an embarrassing pause each time he tried to get them going. (Novy, 1985, p. 123)

Losing his way and meeting with little response, the officer threatened the men with the 'efficiency and discipline' of the German soldier. This entirely understandable act of a nervous lecturer, unable to get a response and uncertain of the topic, does, however, cut right across the purpose of the ABCA discussion. The 'thinking' soldier and raised morale can hardly be threatened into existence. Not surprisingly, soldiers leaving the talk were recorded as saying they were 'treated like a lot of school children' and later referred to a 'nice sleep' or 'a change from work'. However, the observer himself took a longer view. He thought that the officer (being liked) would improve and that the setting was right but the policy was wrong — if it was to stimulate interest they needed 'a different policy, one of truth, current affairs instead of buried phases of the war' (Novy, 1985, p. 124). The early criticism, made by adult educators and others, of the amateurishness of the enterprise would have been fed by an account of this talk. Professional adult educators had expected to be used more fully in the workings of Army education but the Army response was that it had little choice — it needed to turn its officers into educators. Good sense and keenness were taken on over the expertise of the university lecturer. It was argued that apprehensive officers, possibly unwillingly conscripted into education, became good discussion leaders after thorough preparation with their training manuals. 'Good' seems to have been used as an indicator of an honest pragmatism. The history continues:

> Although few of the regional officers had the knowledge, skill or dexterity of the professional, most of them had certain ruder qualities which, in part, made up for many of their failings in style and knowledge. Usually these officers had the good sense to be honest with

their men and to confess that they were not experts but rather taking the chair for a communal meeting. That approach seldom failed and gave the men a confidence in their own ability to join in. (Hawkins and Brimble, 1947, p. 122)

A third image is then provided for Army education: neither Balliol nor a Leveller's army but rough-and-ready officers, hard-working amateurs who turned themselves into democratic discussion leaders. This third image may explain the emphasis on a Cromwellian New Model Army as seen by Army chiefs of staff as opposed to the Leveller debates. The same image is viewed from a different angle. Its success in practice can then be measured, in part, by the way it trained a specialist group of teachers to run the education programme themselves, overcoming their nervousness or lack of sophistication and supporting them within a framework of ideas on pedagogy and content which allowed them to develop. In some ways this model of the officer as a facilitator of group discussion, which took place under Army discipline, must also have acted as a critique of other ways of being an officer. It could have become a form of in-service evaluation and reappraisal of the task of being an officer while still being one. It is hardly credible that a successful and developing education officer should not have used the skills of the discussion group elsewhere in the role of officer. Certainly there is evidence that many officers took the work as an opportunity for their own self-education (Hawkins and Brimble, 1947, p. 123).

Special training was also offered to many officers by means of weekend courses held in the universities or at the Army School of Education in Wakefield, or at Coleg Harlech (which had been taken over as an Army school of education). Here the course was of five days' duration, the intake consisting of education officers and commanding officers, and the curriculum consisting of lectures about discussion groups and practice in discussion leadership. In the Middle East, the School of Education was continually in movement as its three or four members of staff crisscrossed the different army units of the area, giving lectures and training courses. However, those officers who had received special training were in the minority, and very few commanding officers were involved at all. In the main, then, education officers were self-taught, training themselves by running the groups.

In late 1942, Army education added a further programme of education, still in work time, which was based on the same principles of discussion but which raised a further problem, going beyond questions of amateurishness and self-training. The new programme involved time set aside for advanced skills in soldiering (such as mathematics or map reading), for general studies or correspondence courses, and for Citizenship classes. It was the latter, known as The British Way and Purpose, dealing with the responsibilities of citizens in a democracy, which raised the questions of politics, and of propaganda, in the Army. Earlier comparisons, made with Cromwell's army, can appear to be rhetoric, but The British Way and Purpose, later bound within a single volume, dealt firstly with aspects of the British Way of Life; these included the relations between central and local government, economic policy after the war, the social services and education. The next pamphlets dealt with the Empire and Britain's relations with the world. The rather headlong rush through these subjects was then halted briefly before the same subjects were reviewed in more detail. For instance, Education and the Citizen dealt with education in a democracy, partnership and provision, mixed schooling and models of teaching, while The Responsible Citizen discussed freedom and control, public opinion, activity in politics and religion, etc. The whole course lasted for eighteen months initially, but it was then used as a regular part of Army education, even in the 'release' period, post-war.

Unit instructors found controversy in the later sections on the Empire when a fundamental issue, such as the colour bar, was not discussed. The handling of controversial subjects was a point already stressed by ABCA training, but it was the content of particular sections of The British Way and Purpose, seen as official documents, which now created problems. (In fact the discussion of controversial material and the role of the teacher pre-dates the later humanities curriculum programme [HCP] of the 1970s, although ABCA never worked out detailed guidelines as to procedure.) Bias was regarded as likely to be present in the material or in the leader or in the group's one-sided discussion. There was a concern about the lack of knowledge or lack of group experience an officer might have, but it was felt that practice improved the standard of discussion. This commonsense approach seems to have been justified by the practice of many groups — it was said later that although a discussion on citizenship might have appeared as an invitation to anarchy 'to those who dislike change the most dangerous thing about the group, had they attended it, might have been the speed with which doctrinaire vagueness and oratorical cliche disappeared. They would also have been surprised by the wealth of inside knowledge of civic and municipal activity and of organization of shop and factory which gave the discussions an extremely practical air' (Hawkins and Brimble, 1947, pp. 127–8). The 'good sense and practice' model relies heavily on the good intentions of those involved. The use by the group of its own resources is an argument one removed from the early descriptions of ABCA, to remove the ignorance about the war, but still close to the rhetoric of a 'thinking' soldier, and perhaps to the metaphor of the university tutorial.

The Radical Metamorphosis

While the ideal of the practical discussion, sharpening its analytical procedures and carefully handling controversial issues, was a common image of the histories of the wartime education programmes, there is also evidence that the Cromwellian New Model Army was being influenced by its own Levellers and 'Agitators', and scholarly discourse was being replaced by radical discussions on social and political change. From the early days, the question of the politics of the citizen army was being raised. An early group was described at the time as having a 'practical' interest in education, but practical meant that it was largely politics. The men felt that our only chance of survival, as a nation, was in saner and wiser politics than we had known for many years. They wanted to know what kind of world would be theirs when the Second World War had finished, and how they would reconstruct the happiness that had vanished (Hawkins and Brimble, 1947, p. 129).

This was a group led by an Oxford don, again representing the influence of the idea of the liberal education, but the search for a practical politics was on in many groups. The British Way and Purpose allowed civilians and other ranks, as well as officers, to act as group leaders or instructors. A different perspective on the rise of Army education, laying less emphasis on liberal education, and more on the radical movement, is given by Kisch in his book The Days of the Good Soldiers. The rhetoric of the New Model Army is given a sharp twist. Describing the transfusion of new blood into Army education, he writes:

Teachers, university graduates and other professionals scrambled to get in. It was an opportunity for which many pre-war activists from the labour, trade union and anti-fascist movements had hoped, but hardly expected. (Kisch, 1985, p. 10)

Kisch describes a series of events, related to the reorganizing of the Ninth Army, under Montgomery, and in the large military bases in Egypt, with contingents of soldiers from all over Europe, which created a radical upsurge based around the structures and content of the ABCA and British Way and Purpose programmes. Many soldiers, activists in the Commonwealth Party or the Labour or Communist Parties, worked together, even unofficially and clandestinely, as a radical education network, a group of Levellers within the Cromwellian Army. This parallel is directly possible since the Putney Debates of the Civil War Levellers were mirrored in the Mock Parliament of Cairo. The Mock Parliament was a not uncommon idea, pre-war, occurring in schools or in civic education, but in Cairo it was distinguished from early ABCA customs by being organized by the other ranks. On its organizing committee were Communist Party members and trade union activists, and the ABCA education officer was a known radical educationist. The Parliament grew in attendance as its radical bills attracted attention — in the first session, a bill to nationalize the distributive trades was passed by an overwhelming majority, and there was standing room only. Very soon, an election, taken among the 500 in attendance, voted in 'Labour' with a clear majority. Soon after, the Force's Parliament was dissolved by the military authorities in Cairo, but not before a debate at Westminster about whether King's Regulations could be amended to allow off-duty soldiers to engage in political activity. The Army Council rejected this and at the same time posted many of the leaders of the Parliament elsewhere. Yet the idea of the Parliament could so easily have been one of the suggestions made to interest soldiers in current affairs and education in the ABCA hand-book, along with films, wall newspapers, quizzes, etc. What makes it import-ant here is that it revealed, in a single but dramatic case, the radicalization of the soldier-citizen's opinion. The soldiers were interested in education now to the extent that they were apparently breaking Army discipline (in a significant way, for some officers) and acting as an engine for radical social and political change in the UK. Early parallels with the New Model Army were beginning to be distinctly worrying to Army Command.

Another episode in the politics of ABCA occurred when the Beveridge Report on social security, national health and employment was published in the UK. Although it was highly publicized, Churchill's government was embar-rassed by the popularity of its proposals. A summary of the report, produced by Beveridge for ABCA, was withdrawn by the War Office in December 1942, two days after its publication. This not only angered the soldiers but was seen by many people as a sign of the Government's bad faith towards the Beveridge plans. The summary was banned for three months. Kisch describes the un-official circulation of the plans in the Middle East army. A civilian leader of an Army British Way and Purpose discussion group in England described the ban's effect on his group:

> there is a universal demand amongst the men for discussion of the Beveridge Report. It is the one subject they are all clamouring to hear about. In the Army discussion group for which I am responsible we are staging a full-dress discussion of it in the near future, and are not a bit concerned what the official opinion of the War Office is about it. (Mass Observation Archive, 16 December 1942)

So, although there was increased sensitivity in the War Office and in Army Command as to the politics of ABCA and The British Way and Purpose, there appeared to be a degree of ignorance as to the widespread interest in the post-war society discussed regularly by the troops, in and out of the discussion groups. The Mass Observer was, initially, deeply suspicious of the kind of free discussion likely to take place in ABCA, especially when he had heard that in some local military camps these were taking place after the soldiers' hours of duty, but an invitation to talk to some local soldiers changed his mind. They expressed themselves with 'vigour and vehemence':

> these men had a very good idea of what they wanted after the war and seemed determined to get it. Equality of opportunity, a basic minimum wage on which a man can raise a family and share in re-sponsibility in industry. They realise that many of the things they want won't be obtainable without a bitter struggle against vested interests and they realised that if enough of them want the same thing badly enough and are willing to organise, they can get it. (Mass Observation Archive, 4 April 1942)

The ideas they held are a particular expression of the sort of ideas and information present within The British Way and Purpose — partnership and democratic responsibility, etc. — but they had been sharpened by the context in which they were received. It is not that the rules of discussion or an officer's interest in education were irrelevant, but, as in the Middle East, the soldiers had a strong, natural interest in the post-war reconstruction. The Mass Observer reports the way the same soldiers, now attending his British Way and Purpose discussion group in the town, were concentrating on the government's intentions as to demobilization and employment, even before the Beveridge debacle, and were bitter and sceptical about the government. At a debate in mid-1942, nobody, in a group of thirty, spoke in the government's favour. Nine months later, the Observer, a teacher, says: 'I wish these gentlemen [of the War Office] could hear the sort of things the troops say in the army discussion group I hold every week' (Mass Observation Archive, 23 January 1943).

Army Education and Curriculum History

Army education in the form of the Army Bureau of Current Affairs and the British Way and Purpose programme was a major feature of a large citizen's army during the Second World War. The focus of its work was current affairs and social reconstruction and its processes were drawn liberal and adult education. For many of the soldiers, airmen and navy personnel who had been educated in elementary schools pre-war, the style and content of the curriculum must have been quite new. The intensity of the process, which undoubtedly occurred in many units, cannot have been equalled for them by any peacetime experience of education (in its widest sense).

However, while curriculum history may develop as an area of study to encompass non-school experiences and programmes or to trace influences on the school curriculum, its problems multiply when the actuality of educational experience and its effects are taken as the focus for research. Like the *Handbook of Suggestions for Schools*, published for elementary schools for the first fifty years of this century, The British Way and Purpose was the handbook for this curriculum innovation. Yet, however strict in its application it was intended to be, it is fallible as a source of reliable information about what went on in Army education. It tells us much about the intentions of its sponsors and the opinions of writers, even about the style and ideology of coalition or consensus politics within a progressive frame. Certainly it is possible to make comparisons and develop congruences between the ideas of The British Way and Purpose and the policies of the immediate post-war period, but it is quite another problem to suggest that the effectiveness of The British Way and Purpose in practice lay in producing these effects. However striking the appeal of the ABCA propaganda films, the same problem applies — what was Army education like in practice? If this question is not asked, then curriculum history is just another form of administrative history.

The images of Army education form another avenue by which to explore its actuality. Paradoxically, the image, or, in reality, the several images of the programme, allow a tension or contradiction to develop which creates an opportunity for the reader to produce hunches or make guesses as to the problems of practice. The contrasting images of the liberal university and the Model Army might appear united in a period when equality of educational opportunity moved in from the margins or when patriotism allowed nationalism to override other contradictions, but these images can never quite be made homologous. The Army was to be like a permanent university extension class, debating and discussing, in the process of building a 'weapon of the mind' in all its soldiers. As Balliol produced its cadres for the administrative class at home and in the Empire, so the Model Army was produced to be the backbone of the Protectorate's administration. For a moment these images almost join together. Yet in the Britain of the mid-1940s and in its armies, the products of Balliol and the heirs of the Model Army were in different ranks. The Model Army is an image still used by the Left as one of its own, while Balliol is a touchstone for the Right. In conversation the two are not joined but have separate lives in separate discourse. Earnest adults in conversation are not joined by the image of earnestness alone but by the purpose of their conversation. While the two images appeared more or less simultaneously in descriptions of the education programme, it is hard not to arrange them chronologically or even geographically, suggesting that the Model Army was a later, more radical development, or even a Middle East phenomenon. Even a pedagogical framework fits, moving from the early scheme of visiting speakers to that of the discussion group, to suggest that the actuality of the process became more like the Model Army. In practice the images represent educational traditions that were probably both present at the same time in all the education programmes, constituting a permanent source of contradiction between officers and other ranks or between one base and another. The image intended and the image perceived can be different. Historical commentators, like Kisch, talk of the new Levellers, further extending the Model Army metaphor and also subverting it, for the Levellers or the Diggers were not intended consequences of either programme, in the seventeenth or the twentieth centuries. Evidence of the Levellers in operation is there though it is either localized or specific to a particular group. Other images can be retrospectively applied, such as that of the first democratic university, a precursor of the universities of the 1960s or the Open University. Or is a curriculum innovation, like the Humanities Project, a possibility? The advice offered on the operation of discussion groups bears a striking resemblance to that created in the early 1970s for the HCP.

There is also evidence of failure. This only leaks out in footnotes within enthusiastic or official histories of Army education. The Mass Observer was most upset by a friend in the RAF who persisted in writing him letters about the apathy in his unit towards education and post-war reconstruction. The success of the operation depended upon developing an administrative network for distance learning and upon training officers to teach. Success was dependent upon the commanding officer as this example shows:

> the brigadier expressed no desire to meet the lecturer . . . and no commanding officer appeared for the visit of four days. The lecturer was not surprised, therefore, to find little enthusiasm among the men — an empty information room, or empty army educational centre and a first lecture attended by four men while thousands were kicking their heels outside. (Hawkins and Brimble, 1947, p. 296)

The ideas of adult education might have been anathema to some commanding officers. Army education might have been seen as disruptive of order and discipline or unnecessary or too bothersome to organize. It might have appeared to be something very much apart from their main responsibility for military efficiency, even though its creators saw it as providing a positive impetus for efficiency. In its official or semi-official histories the programmes were declared to be successes and they were in the sense that these histories were describing them, that is as a major logistical operation. The resistance of commanding officers was not spotlighted nor would one expect it to be in this type of record.

What were the experiences of the teaching officers? Very few of them had been trained in residential short courses, more had been in direct contact with a travelling support unit (for the Middle East), and most of them appeared to have trained themselves. This is acceptable for an innovation that has been designed to be applied by a teacher, however ineffective this might be in reality, but this innovation was supported by the idea of the supportive, facilitating teacher-officer. What support mechanism existed for these officers and how did they cope with this challenging role, in many cases an official sanctioning of a new direction for them, not just for for the soldiers? Did these officers try to bypass this threat to their role as 'expert' and 'commander' and, if not, how did they manage a 'facilitating' and a 'leadership' role and were these roles incompatible? Who supported these teachers? How willing or able were they to use their handbook in developing discussion skills or to read the regular pamphlets to supplement their knowledge of the issues? How did they cope with resistant soldiers who would act under orders but could not be made to participate in discussions? It is this issue, addressed within the competing images, that is at work in the actuality of the discussions. How did the officer develop the culture of the university discussion? How did the soldiers discuss under orders or develop a negotiated order within the discussion reflecting the ideas of the Model Army? The Directorate of the education programme seems to have been distanced from its working deliberations. How did they gather intelligence about its progress? If discipline needed to be defended, then the local commander would deal with 'extremism' by transferring soldiers at short notice elsewhere. An impression is gained that the vitality and urgency of the discussions taking place among units of the forces was not 'known' to the Directorate. Perhaps their success in creating and expanding a massive education programme — and adult education had never been organized on this scale before — occupied them fully. They had to defend it against charges of being conservative and inadequately organized in its early years and, presumably, against being a left-wing plot at the end.

If it was a success it was because the content of its work, especially in the social reconstruction pamphlets of The British Way and Purpose, was in line with the needs of the armed forces, which were beginning to move onto the offensive and to consider the post-war world. By this standard, it later became a goal to many of the units who took ideas of political change and citizenship beyond the coded and limited aspect of their British Way and Purpose appearance. It became a Model Army despite the call and the programme designed to make it one. To an extent, this was due to the spirit of the times, the *Zeitgeist*, which was embedded in the citizen's army as a dissatisfaction with the old order and the politicians, generals and class hierarchies of that order. The programme gave these soldiers, to a greater or lesser degree, the chance to work out their ideas with each other on the future of the post-war society and discuss freely, within and without the group, the politics of social change. They made it a Model Army, taking that message or image forward beyond its initial usage, even beyond the original understanding of its originators. The programme carried more messages, about discussion and society, than its writers were aware of. It was received within a strong spirit of change and search for knowledge, in many places; the climate had changed. It was created to save and reconstruct an army but it was disseminated at a period of gradual military success. The content took on a new meaning, no longer explaining a past society and how it worked; it was discussed as a blueprint for a reconstructed society.

Blumer, in his critique of The Polish Peasant, made some points of value in relation to this memo on curriculum history. He argued, in relation to a much more complete form of primary historical record, that it is useful in 'suggesting leads, in enabling insight and in helping to frame more fruitful questions' (Blumer, 1979, p. 80). It certainly raises many questions for me. The first set is to do with the programme's operation, its activity: how did the discussions work? One criterion for judging its effectiveness must be the quality of the discussion process and the political meanings that were represented in them. This would need a form of oral history project, or to develop it further, the beginnings of a cultural history of social experience. The second set relates to its images. How are images selected and promoted? It is hard to 'see' Army education without being influenced by the way it was described at the time in its official descriptions or in official or social histories of a later period. Again, finding out the process by which army education was developed within its headquarters and then produced for consumption could take place within an elite oral history, a rare object. My discussion of the images could be extended within an approach suggested by Richard Johnson in his essay (1986) on cultural studies. His writing on social texts makes the point that texts or forms are themselves representations and that they may have competing meanings in other social practices. My use of the idea of constant contradiction in the programme is congruent with his approach as is the necessity of identifying dominant and subordinate readings of the text. The third set of questions is related to the effects of this programme. Within it lay possibilities for relating the idea of the post-war consensus to an education programme, that is to point up the way its ideas and procedures surface in post-war discussions on the new universities, the development of local education authority policies and the whole idea of partnership, a mixed economy and an active citizenry. On a grand scale this is a question of relating curriculum purposes and processes to a post-war social movement and ideology. Relating, in both cases, does not mean arguing for physical linkages (though it may do in the careers of significant elite members) but for the interrelation in contra-dictory or supportive processes of understandings, congruencies and homologies between the programme and post-war Britain. This memo ends with a last note to its writer that curriculum history could be like a version of cultural studies: a form of structural analysis and of cultural production within history.

5　Social Constructions of Quality in Teaching

> What is expected of schools alters over time with changes in society and in national circumstances. In consequence, successive generations may differ in how they define standards at school, and how they measure changes in such standards. (DES, 1985)

The above quotation is drawn from the introduction to a major policy reform of the 1980s which focused on teaching quality (DES, 1985). In the context of the policy document it was quickly made and then passed over in the rush to policy details. Yet in the quotation there are a number of possibilities raised about how expectations of schools (and so, of teachers) have altered and as a consequence of this, the idea of the teacher has altered.[1] Indeed for the purposes of this essay it introduces the notion of changed expectations about and successive definitions of teaching quality very well. There cannot be a useful definition of teacher quality which transcends its context. Strong definitions about teacher quality are most prone to ahistoricism and arguments that use them tend to assertion not argument. Most policy documents which are relevant to this area tend not to argue for their view of teacher quality so much as they content themselves with a self-evident description.

Although the *Better Schools* quotation has its value, as it introduces the time/context specificity of the definition of the teacher, it does not help much with an exploration of how these changes occur, nor which agency or department implements them, nor how cohesive the idea of a 'generation' is? There is little sense of the reality of the different definitions or the tensions or contradictions which exist within that reality or generation at one time. These questions are all the more interesting as *Better Schools* was itself the harbinger of massive structural changes in schooling, the economy of education and teachers' work which have not yet finished. However this quotation allows us to recognize that teacher quality (like schooling) cannot be effectively discussed if it is defined reductively, ahistorically or in an essentialist manner. Policy makers or policy influencers may feel able to describe the times the teacher and the task in these ways but this essay will attempt to ground the idea of teacher quality into different specific contexts and show how the idea itself has altered dramatically. Teacher quality has been a contested concept, it is certainly not neutral or self-evident. Definitions have not just emerged or been accepted. Particular social and political circumstances and dominant employer or employee versions have shaped the idea. In the particular case of the *Better Schools* proposals for teacher reform, it would be shortsighted to take a statement on societal changes and the description of necessary policy changes at face value, as the quotation suggests we should. The years of conflict with teachers which preceded the policy paper, the dispute with local education authorities and the radical governmental agenda at the time gave birth to that paper and it was produced by only one party to the dispute, the Government. The Department of Education's version of national circumstance and school change became the dominant one. There was nothing self-evident about it. The attempt to reduce debates about school values and purposes by the imposition of lists of technical, curriculum and managerial duties and skills and to define a new generational standard need to be judged in the context in which they were created. Defining and managing teacher quality, by the standard of *Better Schools* alone, should be treated as a contested and contradictory act.

In this essay I will make reference to four different periods when clear definitions of teacher quality can be seen.[2] These periods are arbitrary, showing, as they do, different perspectives on quality which have operated this century in the state elementary (later the primary and secondary) sector. These periods are viewed in terms of the image of the teacher which policy makers, acting as employers or management advisers, have created, or which managers and management policies have operated. These periods are not produced chronologically to develop an argument on how the image of the 'good' teacher changed but patterns emerged in which the necessity to develop new images of the 'good' teacher resulted from teacher shortages and a redefinition of the purpose of state education and that there were competing definitions of the new teacher. Teaching quality is seen here as a social construction, an attempt to make visible and explicit the practical and ideological management imperatives in any given period. However, the social construction of teacher quality is a contested process; initiatives are taken in response to shortages or emerge out of particular political and social conjunctions which are then responded to by teachers. Generations of teachers are themselves divided, containing as they do, competing practices, favoured 'good teacher' models and biographically ordered work experience around which teachers organize or group.

The periods I have looked at are drawn from research projects I have undertaken in the history and sociology of teachers' work: they are the First World War and the 1920s; the Second World War and the 1940s; the early 1960s and the 1980s. These projects were not intended to develop into a twentieth century history of State–teacher relations and are used here only to make the argument for the social construction of the notion of teacher quality.

The Right Sort of Quality

Looking backwards from the 1990s our perspective on teacher quality might emphasize the reductive and taxonomic aspects of teacher skills which have come to dominate references to quality in Britain, and have been shaped by its current high policy profile. Yet in the early decades of this century, there was less emphasis on technical skills in teaching and more emphasis on the social and political character of the teacher (Lawn, 1987). Teacher quality appears to have been defined in practice in relation to the 'social order', and it was the employer the Government and the local squirearchy which decided what that natural 'social order' was and how teachers either fitted into it or disrupted it and where they should be recruited from to service it. Arguments about the quality of the teaching force at this time were arguments about politics, gender and class.

Managers expected to manage and from schools to local boards or education committees the first two decades are full of reference to the requirements they had for 'their' teachers. They expected to control recruitment policies, employment tenure, job responsibilities and aspects of teachers' social existence. Their expectation was one of absolute control over their employees. This might vary from in rural areas, teachers' politics, churchgoing, and social life, to in urban areas, their right to manage and the power of teachers to combine. At local level, school managers, representing local ratepayers (business class, farmers, etc.) constantly examined their teachers — on their drinking, their chapel-going, their politics and their associations, and so forth. They judged the quality of their teachers against their definition of the natural 'social order' and their place as managers in operating on behalf of that order.

Neither they nor the central government expected teachers to cavil at the creation of new routes into teaching or the creation of new classes of skilled and unskilled teachers or their recruitment of, in times of shortage or because of economies or strikes, any person they saw fit to be a teacher. As far as they were concerned quality was signified less by particular skills than by social and political representations, that is, what did the teacher appear to be? Which class were they recruited from? Did they accept the conditions of their work? Were they the right sort of people? This attitude can be viewed from the correspondence in local newspapers and recorded accounts or council and committee meetings during strikes, disruption or policy changes; it can also be read in examples culled by writers who began to treat this subject as one of civil liberties or of class oppression. Another source is the number of commentaries, from the turn of the century onwards, which make reference to the worrying rise in this large group of secular, influential and educated workers and the power they might wield in their communities.

Teachers were recruited mainly from the working class. In reviewing the pupil–teacher system, in 1902, the Board of Education referred to the origins of this system (Board of Education, 1907). It was intended to be a cheap system of recruitment to elementary schools, drawn from the children of the manual labour class, and until the Revised Code came, it worked (at that time mangers appointed 'anybody' to get the State grant). By 1898, it was stated that this method of recruitment was becoming 'economically wasteful and educationally unsatisfactory and even dangerous . . .' The newly created importance of the education system and a 'well-equipped body of teachers' meant that direct recruitment from the labouring classes was now inappropriate. It was suggested that they be encouraged to enter secondary education, gaining a liberal education which might overcome their 'narrowness of intellectual and professional outlook'. Social class and economic efficiency ran together. These teachers had sufficient quality at the right cost to the taxpayer when the demands on state elementary education were minimal. As this system began to be seen as economically useful to the industrial society and not just a drain on it, then quality was redefined. It would be the same class but with a longer education. The difference between the Revised Code period, when untrained teachers were recruited from the manual classes, and later, was a reflection on the changing economic purpose of state education but the tension continued between teacher quality defined by cheapness and by economic purpose. This continued and explains the proliferation of routes into teaching and the rise of a teacher association, fuelled by social grievances and contradictory training policies. Quality was a relative term, suited to employer purpose, and contested by organized teachers who took a consistent line on craft skill and training (expressed as professionalism, Lawn, see Chapter 5).

The recruitment of women teachers in increasing numbers in the later nineteenth century and early twentieth century is a reflection of this need to reduce costs and to increase efficiency, a conundrum produced by their need to train the labouring class more to teach in elementary schools. One way was to recruit women teachers — the London School Board, opposing the recruitment of untrained teachers argued

> (that) it has been made a matter of regret that the teachers of elementary children have to be drawn from a class of society which, to say the least, are in early life not surrounded by refining influences. The better prospects offered to teachers by the extension of school boards are far more likely to attract a higher class of women than a higher class of men. It is well known that there is a considerable number of women, socially raised above the labouring class, who suffer much privation through the scarcity of remunerative labour suited to their capacities . . . (Copelman, 1985, p. 94)

Class is interlinked with gender in defining teacher quality. As men were seen as being able to operate in a wider labour market and to have higher economic value, teaching quality was soon defined as being related to women. Women would be more inclined to teach, they would have the right qualities and they would also be available at the right price. They would also be judged on their ability to teach a newly gender differentiated curriculum, in particular the domestic economy element, including needlework. Although the argument for the recruitment of women into teaching was to develop nationally, a permanent tension developed between the idea of the 'amateur' lady teacher and the reality of a large, overworked, underpaid force of women teachers;

between the idea of intellectual work and skilled/unskilled labour and between rates of pay divided according to gender not equal labour. While their work was valued it was not valued as much as men's work. Promotion, a sign of quality, was mainly available to men. Quality was subdivided by gender.

Further, teaching quality was defined by its conservatism. In the First World War period and immediately afterward, the involvement by teachers in Labour Party politics was viewed by local managers and ratepayers, and central government, as a sign of social disruption or even social danger (Lawn, 1987a). While this movement in labour politics can be overstated, it varied in depth and value, it was viewed with concern even amid the general social unrest. Teachers were seen as significant in the reproduction of the social order. While they were also not part of it (by membership) they were seen as acting on behalf of those who were. The notion of teacher discontent was not so easily coped with as it was in earlier days when the state education system was not so important economically. The result of the strikes and political action by many teachers was the creation of a new policy on teacher quality by the government and H.A.L. Fisher at the Board of Education. Fisher heightened and changed the idea of the 'good teacher'; he argued for 'an efficient and devoted corps of teachers' who would produce good citizens, be patriotic and apolitical, and realise the benefits to society of the projected investment in education (Lawn 1987a, p. 66). Fisher described a system of self-government for teachers based on professionalism, responsibility and collegiality. Most of all, he talked of a time when there would be higher standards of education and training for teachers. Fisher was battling against the ideas of various socialist writers, Labour Party and union leaders and workers who were offering teachers a different vision of their role and work in the future. In this sense he was developing a new version of teacher quality, an ideology to produce a policy. The ideas of teacher quality he provided, distinctive as they were and contrastive with the past, were made to recruit and retain teachers, literally and figuratively, to a new state policy. Teachers were redefined; they would have self-government and not petty restrictions, they would be educated not just semi-trained, they would be professionals not just hired hands. Teaching quality was redefined because the importance of the education industry had been raised and because their value as state professionals had been recognized. The concept of the social order, expressed as a cultural and social hierarchy and as an economic project, was important to teaching. Teachers were measured against that idea and were seen as a social danger if they did not match up to it because of their actions or sometimes because of who they were. On the other hand, the 'good teacher' was probably not in a national association of teachers (or not active within the association), not antagonistic to managers and their control over conditions of work, not politically or socially radical and accepting of the class/gender basis on which they were employed. In this period, teaching quality appears to have been mainly defined by reductive class, gender or political attributes in relation to state or local labour markets and 'social order'; teaching skills were not so much technical as social. Not until the mid-1920s did a major teacher training route emerge which represented features of Fisher's ideological policy.

The New Look in the 1940s

The Second World War was followed by a period in which an argument about new kinds of teacher can be seen clearly against the backdrop of older elementary school realities. This post-war period, often described as one of consensus or central–local partnership, or even 'indirect rule' (Lawn and Ozga, 1986) followed a wartime emergency in schools, and contained a radical reconstruction in the aftermath of the 1944 Education Act. The shift in the argument about teacher quality took place against the problem of recruitment in teaching, the creation of emergency training routes and a commission which tried to establish a new teacher education structure, linking colleges and universities together. This time though there was an emphasis on the 'good teacher' experimenting and the mythology of a distinctive English tradition of teacher autonomy and professionalism appears to be rooted in the 1940s.

Teachers' work had changed in wartime. Women teachers had again shouldered the work of the education industry (Lawn, 1987b). Teachers' workload had grown enormously due to the use of schools as places of emergency social care in the war; schools had been used as salvage centres, emergency centres for feeding and housing blitzed families, rest centres and distributors of clothing coupons. Their working hours and conditions had changed and because of war disruption, their work had become harder; it was harder to get the same results from children.

Teachers had become quasi-civil servants and schools had become part of a wartime, and later post-war, social welfare administration. The Welfare State was built in education out of wartime needs and priorities. Schools were used for medical inspection and care and provided a milk and meals service. Kenneth Richmond described this change in the nature and importance of schooling to the State, and the consequent changes in the definition of teaching so,

> (the elementary teacher) gained some insight in to the meaning of social service; he was becoming a welfare officer in the best sense of the word. True he detested this metamorphosis; protested that 'he didn't know what things were coming to'; felt that his status was being degraded to that of an odd-job man, forever at the beck and call of pestering officials; but there was no gainsaying his broadened outlook. (Richmond, 1945, p. 134)

H.C. Dent, the editor of *The Times Educational Supplement*, at the time, asked the same question:

> (All these developments) have combined with other wartime developments in the educational situation to present the teachers with a pretty

— and embarrassing — problem: what is the teacher's job? Is it to teach or to do a multitude of other jobs as well? (Dent, 1944, p. 161)

Teacher quality had become more broadly defined. The primary pastoral role was becoming established and the teacher worked in a site which was extending its functions and required new skills. New wartime responsibility led to increased levels of innovation in the curriculum and a recognition that this was now the area of teacher competence and responsibility. These gains came with some losses. The time for this changed work, in curriculum and in pastoral care, came out of the teacher's life, the working day was extended in practice. The function of the job incorporated school supervisory tasks, including meal supervision. Men and women reacted in different ways to these events and in some school sectors what was rejected by some was an opportunity for others. A new definition of the teacher was created in which teaching time was described and controlled by the employer yet the teacher was valued and had a responsibility, built upon the major role schools now had in a society reconstructing.

The creation of a special training route into teaching in the mid-1940s altered the idea of teaching quality once again. The shortage of teachers had led to the creation of a scheme to recruit demobilized soldiers. The Ministry of Education was faced with a shortfall in the number of teachers due to the raising of the school-leaving age and the other developments associated with the 1944 Education Act. Although training colleges operated a two-year certificate course for post-school entrants, which was about to be raised to three years, the emergency scheme proposed was based on an intensive one-year course (followed by a two-year study/probation period). The Ministry of Education leased or requisitioned suitable sites across the country and began to train teachers itself.

Acceptance into emergency teacher training was based upon age (between 21–35), war service, a school certificate (or a subject essay) and a judgment as to suitability for teaching according to 'temperament, personality and intellectual capacity' (Ministry of Education, 1950, p. 23). The judgment of the interview boards was used to develop the common idea of the standard required of a 'qualified teacher'. As Dent pointed out (Dent, 1942, p. 20), in a brief summary of this scheme, the main reason for its success was the 'maturity, enthusiasm and hard work of the students'. This is the image of teacher quality prevailing in this period. It was a question of experience, no longer one of class, gender or qualification. The image is both apt and spurious. It was a recognition of the influence of the Army education programme which produced motivated people with an interest in education (Lawn 1989) and it was a post-hoc rationalization of the need to create an emergency non-standard entry.

In an official description and evaluation of the scheme, the new Ministry of Education described the quality of the students as being the significant feature of the scheme. This quality was specified as 'keenness and sinlessness of purpose', 'a wide range of talents and accomplishments' and 'powers of initiative and organization'. Through the section dealing with students, emphasis is placed on their maturity, responsibility and experience. Maturity was defined as a personal quality and previous experience, related together. Competence in teaching depended upon the following personal attributes it was stated — vitality, genuine interest in one's fellows, conviction of the social importance of schools, willingness (and ability) to consider the problems of teaching from the child's point of view and readiness to reflect on, and profit by, one's own experience. Problems in training could be ascribed to the following personal qualities — a colourless personality, aloofness, complacency and a cynical attitude to teaching (Ministry of Education, 1950, pp. 36–46).

In this way teacher quality was shaped by the idea of maturity, meaning the relationship between experience and personality. This was a key image but it fitted the newly developing idea of teaching as a pastoral or social welfare role, a consequence of wartime and post-war reconstruction. As the Ministry argued, the values of teaching have more meaning for the mature student; if the profession of teaching was of a 'highly social character' then the training of teachers could benefit from mature entrants and would be constituted differently for and by them. It was the quality of their 'personal relationships' with children and colleagues which counted, their eagerness and enthusiasm and their willingness to take on out-of-school activities. This image of teacher quality was both a reflection of a policy response to teacher shortage and of a change in the nature of teaching.

Better Schools: From Newsom to Joseph

The different requirements and interests of the late 1950s and 1960s can be seen within the work of the Central Advisory Council for Education in England, and one of its major publications, the Newsom Report (Half our Future, see CACE, 1963). The focus of the report was the education of the average adolescent pupil in preparation for the raising of the school leaving age. In retrospect, through the composition of the Committee and in its arguments, it can be seen as a link between the emphasis in the 1940s on the welfare and social aspects of education and the later emphasis in the 1980s and 1990s on specialism and teamwork.

The root question which the Report asked and answered was 'what kind of teachers, with what professional and personal resources, do the schools require to do the job?' (CACE, 1963, p. 98). It was not just a severe shortage of teachers with which they were faced, they felt that 'good teachers' needed to be retrained in 'slum, heavy industrial and other ill favoured areas' and that teachers' work should be made or shown to be 'personally and professionally satisfying in its demands'. In its effort to restructure the work of the secondary school teacher to meet the needs of the children, it suggested a new emphasis in these secondary schools on pastoral care, on cross-curricula competency, on extra-school work, on teamwork, on vocationalism and on school support services. As it pointed out, it was trying to produce a new and 'sufficiently attractive professional image' for teachers (CACE, 1963, p. 99). The consequences for teacher education and for the teachers, that is the idea of the 'good teacher', were great. There was to be a move away from the mature, experienced generalist form teacher in the secondary schools; it wasn't the image that was wrong, indeed the report talks about the valuable contribution the mature entrant would make to the 'personal education' of adolescents but the fact that teachers' shortages were more likely to be filled from young entrants who would need particular skills. A new emphasis on skills resulted, concentrating on mastery of two or more subjects, on pedagogical studies (teaching methods and techniques) and on educational studies (sociological and psychological study). The knowledge about these areas would now define teacher quality. The shortage of teachers, and the felt necessity to provide a good education for all British citizens, had led to the creation of a new image of the teacher, built on new craft skills and longer professional training. That image was also a youthful one, it was to be associated with the expansion of higher education in 1960s and the establishment of more comprehensive schools. For a while teacher quality was, in one of its contemporary images, associated with a young comprehensive school teacher, using subject and pedagogical skills. The Newsom idea of professional purpose, associated with the inner-city and industrial areas, was soon developed into a compensatory education approach and positive discrimination in schooling by teachers. In urban areas, as Gerald Grace has shown, this new purpose of teaching, in primary and secondary schools, soon became fractured and different versions of it, liberal and radical, became embedded in the relations between groups of teachers (Grace, 1978).

In the 1980s a new image of teacher quality was developed by the State from the management of policy changes in primary schools. The new generation primary teacher was to be significantly different to her predecessors. They had worked in (what has been described as) a period of educational consensus in which the primary headteacher had a significant practical role in defining the teacher's work which, generally speaking, was classroom-based and generalist. They weren't specialists in a subject area, they worked under the head's direction (tightly or loosely operated) and they were responsible for the children in their classroom/age group.

By the late 1980s it was possible to see clearly the new idea of primary teaching, expressed in government publications, and the new qualities associated with it (HMI, 1985; DES, 1985). The duties, responsibilities and performance of the teacher have become more closely defined. The craft skills of teaching have been codified, subject specialism is a requirement, curriculum content and its assessment have been tightly specified. Teaching has been redefined as a supervisory task, operating within a team of teachers and (probably) with an allowance for leading and managing them, work is related to the overall development plan or whole school management policy. It is argued that

> Professionalism in the primary school has moved on from being class-room-based, usually in isolation from other teachers, fairly well de-fined by the head but in a context of responsibility and autonomy, to a collective school wide job, based on narrowly defined though complex tasks within a context of shared management functions and tight areas of responsibility, clearly defined and appraised. (Lawn, 1988a)

The kinds of personal qualities, once referred to in discussions of mature entrants or within pastoral/welfare aspects of schooling, have moved, in this discourse, from being ideal characteristics to part of a job description in which specified qualities are to become necessary skill requirements.

Quality?

Obviously teaching has altered this century but the focus of this essay has been on the dominant views about teachers and how these views have turned into significant policies. However the emphasis has been less on if or how the policies worked and more on the distinctiveness of the different images of the 'good teacher' produced at different periods. The metaphor of image is not literal; there are dominant views but there are contested views. The sharper the image the less likely it is to be an accurate representation — for my purposes. In this essay the image will have to be in semi-focus.

Why should teaching be redefined and what purpose does talk of quality or the 'good teacher' serve in redefining the teacher's work? It isn't just 'changes' or 'national circumstance' or 'generations', it is the way in which these terms are used to legitimate a shift in the production of teachers and their system of working.

Teacher shortage appears to be linked with either a redefinition of, or a restated emphasis on, teacher quality. This may be to forestall criticism that shortages allow the State to recruit teachers by any route, and by what standard, it so wishes. The personal qualities and experiences of a teacher may be emphasized because of the creation of an alternative training route or because of the need to create new groups of teachers for newly created specialized jobs. Both these assumptions could be developed from the creation of the emergency training route post-war and the college secondary route (Newsom) in the 1960s. Whatever the case, shortage seems to produce redefinition of the teacher's role by the State.

The quality of teachers has been closely associated with their maturity, social class, politics or gender and it has been difficult at times to clearly see the teacher through a perspective which views them in this way. They were to be recruited from the working class for the elementary schools and then from mature entrants for the new secondary general form teacher or primary generalists. Again, it appears to be that quality is redefined according to state purposes; as new sectors of schooling are developed then, as with shortages, the job is redefined to suit groups of probable recruits. At several points, it appears that these recruits are drawn from a pool of untapped labour and the job is redefined to suit their qualities. There is no other teacher quality but their 'personal' qualities and these are almost stereotypically defined. The idea of skill is not consistently emphasized in defined teacher quality, although when it is it alters considerably between cases. It may be loosely referred to or specified in detail, related to classroom control or to pedagogy *ad* curriculum, assumed to be clearly definable or to be discretionary and 'professional'.

Although the State has appeared to be more closely defining teacher quality as the century progresses, there are discrepancies or omissions between definitions. It is sometimes not clear why one view is taken, rather than another, and the definitions sometimes appear expedient. There are also tensions between the ideological view of the teacher and the practice, and between the dominant definition of the 'good teacher' and the teacher's definition.

At the present time, teacher shortage and a major critique of teacher education in policy circles are again creating new images of teacher quality. They appear to range widely at the moment; the National Curriculum Council is suggesting that a school-based initial teacher training should be comprised of subject studies, the National Curriculum and classroom management only and the Centre of Policy Studies and the Hillgate group (on the Right) take a similar view, reducing training to subjects and substituting school teaching apprenticeship for pedagogical and educational studies. The Council for the Accreditation of Teacher Education still seem to prefer a training institution-based-teacher education but with more school-based work, a general move to competency-based training, better coordination of the curriculum and monitoring of quality. There is, within the training institutions and in some local education authorities and schools which work with them, a view of the modern teacher, called the reflective practitioner, which describes a thorough training in a highly-skilled enquiry-based class teaching mode (Pollard and Tann, 1987). The related idea of the effective teacher, promoted by the National Primary Centre, which, using ideas from primary practice and the HMI, see the teacher as constantly reviewing practice and working in teams (NPC, 1989). There are competing images of the teacher in these approaches, mirroring societal changes and ideological perspectives on the role of the teacher. They have been produced within a social and educational context which is deeply divided. Which of these views of teacher quality will prevail, at what level of the system and by what political and policy process? How will the contested notion of teacher quality be temporarily resolved?

Notes

1 This paper is based on a set of short case studies which reveal patterns in the formal or official expectations of teacher quality in the twentieth century. There is little

emphasis in this paper on the teachers' own definitions of quality nor on their struggle to defend these definitions, instead the focus is on the way in which governments altered and shaped the idea of the 'good teacher' to suit their policy purposes. In this paper a full picture is not developed nor is there a causal analysis. It is a first attempt to reveal aspects of the social construction of teacher quality.

2   This paper uses case studies drawn from different historical projects on teachers and teaching which I have undertaken or that I am currently working on. Their focus is always on teachers' work but there have been different emphases. My early work was on teachers' economic conditions, organizations and political alliances but my emphasis today is on the relations between pedagogy, teachers' lives and their labour process. There has been a consequent shift into oral history and ethnographic research in my recent work.

6 Encouraging License and Insolence in the Classroom: Imagining a Pedagogic Shift

It is not uncommon in local museums to find reconstructed classrooms of the past, especially the late Victorian elementary classroom. Rows of uniform seating, slates, a blackboard, a high teacher's desk, a globe and a framed picture or two constitute the classroom. Yet there is a silence in that elementary classroom. What were the routines and the language which inhabited its space? What was its pedagogical order and how was the National Curriculum mediated in its spaces? What was the lived reality of the teacher's work, in and around that classroom?

It is difficult to discern changes in classroom practice even for a qualitative researcher but for an historian it is almost impossible. Fragments of data emerge from footnotes, reminiscences, pamphlets, oral histories, photographs and reports. Their relationship to pedagogical practices is always indistinct. It is easier to date the arrival of a new textbook in a school or suggest the influence of a book on the basis of the copies sold than it is to try to reconstruct the pedagogical order of a classroom, indeed it may be almost impossible. Well intentioned curriculum histories move easily into the narrative derived from administrative accounts and move further away from the classroom when those accounts are based on examining bodies or professional associations. Yet the classrooms of the past are not easily reconstructed and re-lived: the technology of the classroom appears discernible but this is an illusion. The meaning and practice of work to the teacher has gone, along with the culture and politics of their social and educational existence. Social and classroom relationships with pupils and parents have gone. Old crafts and routines are barely knowable. Even oral histories, rare enough in teaching, build a narrative of work and meaning which is not rooted in schoolwork and use unexplained terms (like classroom or desk or lesson) which have no clear meaning out of their time–space context. The issue is not just one of information, of course, but of perspective, the lack of questions raised about the meaning of classroom realities for researchers.

This paper is an attempt to begin a project on the silent social history of the classroom (Silver, 1992), to ask questions about the kind of information and a viable methodology to be used in this project, to look closely at a possible pedagogic shift in the secondary modern school and to raise some questions towards a critique of curriculum history theorizing.

The Idea of a Pedagogical Shift

The project is concerned with the kind of evidence of a new pedagogy, a particular focus in curriculum history, in post-Second World War England, which may be produced or deduced from the fragments and the hegemonic narratives of the time? How can the claim, the argument and the practice be sifted and the realities of classroom pedagogy emerge?

In this paper there is an attempt to explore the rise of a possible pedagogical shift in the state school system, particularly the elementary and (their successor) secondary modern schools, by means of a case study of pedagogical change, through the development of the discussion method in and around schools, in the 1940s and 1950s. The discussion method is threaded through the rhetorical shift taking place in educational writing in the 1940s and later. It is bound together with the reconstruction of society, the building of a new and fairer society, the education of an active citizenship, the new curricula (particularly social studies and civics) and the responsibility of the teacher. The implication is that the package has to be absorbed as whole. At the same time, the method is argued to be the means by which the rest becomes attainable. The citizen, building the new society, will be created in the school through a new technology of teaching, the discussion method; an even newer technology, the professional and well-educated teacher will deliver it.

The idea of the discussion method as a pedagogical shift contains certain assumptions about pedagogy and change. In an important essay on pedagogy, Brian Simon (Simon, 1985) argued that there was no pedagogical tradition in England in the sense that a science of teaching (a pedagogy) embodying both curriculum and methodology (itself systematic knowledge about methods) was produced. The history of pedagogy, as he saw it, was reflected in the lack of interest by the public (private sector) schools and Oxbridge in professional training as they concentrated on assimilation of the pupil into class and culture. The new turn of the century secondary schools used an herbartian framework to classify pupils. This left the elementary schools to develop a pedagogy suitable for a divided schooling and appropriate to their social function. In his essay, Simon treats the idea of pedagogy as a science based on theories about human learning and an attempt to systematically provide a general body of principles about learning and a knowledge about methods of teaching. Theory is treated as the creator of pedagogy which then becomes a systematic exploration of practice. Without the right theory, there can be no fundamental change. It would not be systematic or it would be theoretically flawed etc. 'No pedagogy in England' means therefore no properly theorized and systematically treated approach to learning.

However, in his essay, Simon treats the idea of pedagogy in a further way. He assumes that each structural change to schooling would need a subsequent pedagogic shift but it is not clear what the relation is between a system change and pedagogic one. Presumably, this pedagogic shift will be a response to the new definitions of work and purpose built in to the new structures, for example in relation to the classification of pupils, their assessment, examinations and curriculum. While this shift may be incremental or pragmatic in its development as opposed to theorized and systematic, it is this kind of shift in a system which may be significant in really changing pedagogy rather than an idealized version of theorized change. The idea of discussion as an element in the technology of teaching, that is the procedures, techniques and routines of teaching may be an example of a pedagogic shift in state school teaching.

Technology, an occupational resource, may be derived from a theorized relation to practice and so may imply a systematic practical art (and in that sense it overlaps with the idea of a systematic pedagogy). In teaching it can be argued that the social and work space for the creation of a technology is greater than in many other kinds of work. The consequences of that work space is that it is likely to be a teacher theorizing about practice, rather than a given bureaucratic or centralized version of theory and practice, which is produced. As teachers are not socially neutral, then the theories or formulation of practice will be affected by their social ideas, workplace and the education service (as an organized system or particular kind of work). So this inquiry is focused upon the ideas and practices of teaching and the social influences and work conditions which affect their teaching technologies. From this perspective on technology/pedagogy, pedagogical change follows social change or is a reflection of it. Pedagogy is not technical though it may be reduced to, or include, technicalities (i.e. method) and it would change in response to new social and work needs (new kinds of school etc.) managed by social actors (teachers).

In the relative absence of teacher accounts of pedagogy in their elementary classrooms the images or discourses of education form another avenue by which to explore classroom actuality. Paradoxically, the image, or, in reality, the several images of teaching, allow a tension or contradiction to develop which creates an opportunity for the reader to produce hunches or make guesses as to the possibilities of practice. It is this approach I intend to take here.

Sources of information on practice have to be sought and questioned and in this case, they comprise two internally consistent sets of argument about change in classrooms, produced by major educational writers of the period, and a series of extracts, drawn from 1950s novels, written by teachers, about their classrooms and schools. Both kinds of information may well be fiction yet both may be read against and with each other to produce possibilities for further enquiry, a re-examination of hypotheses about change, and a critical scholarship in the history of education about the silences in the explanation about work. Discontinuities and contradiction could become a way of developing fields of work and levels of interpretation in history of the curriculum.

Post-war Changes

Wartime books on education and society, trying to create an agenda for post-war change, produced a language of community and democracy, sometimes using a liberal elitist adaptation of Christian thought, which appeared to act as the ideological license for a new educational system and practice. Viz.

> Schools have always been provided for (the public or mass) from above, in a form and with a content of studies that suited the ruling interests. It is not surprising, then, that the avowed purpose of such schools until quite recently was to induce usefulness rather than culture. Existing popular culture was wholly set aside as idle and trivial, and the utilizable skills of reading, writing and arithmetic together with simple craftwork and much moral teaching (with a strong emphasis on the nature of obedience) provided the staple . . . The Charity schools of the 17thC and the 18thC and elementary schools of the 19thC were all alike devoted to the same end, and the elementary school of today, struggling towards a more adequate cultural conception . . . is still under (this influence). (Clarke, 1940, p. 30)

Books emerge discussing a new practical, local and civic education; curriculum areas such as social studies or civics were promoted in the new state secondary modern schools (where pupils went if they failed their tests at 11 years of age). Two authors in particular stand out in this period for the extent of their publications about the new practice of education in the secondary modern schools, Harold Dent and Harold Foulkes.

The context from which they wrote about the future was based upon the past, not unreasonably. Dent refers to the pre-war Hadow report (1926) when trying to describe a new modern education

> The general aim should therefore be to offer the fullest possible scope to individuality, while keeping steadily in view the claims and needs of the society in which every individual citizen must live. (Dent, 1942, pp. 146–7)

But Dent referred also to the contemporary influence of the experiment in universal adult education in the armed forces.

> (It was) shown beyond a shadow of a doubt that men and women in all stations of life are hungering for opportunities of increasing their knowledge, skill and understanding. Its most recent development, the Army Bureau of Current Affairs, (ABCA), may yet prove to be the long sought answer to the question of political education. The growing popularity of wireless discussion groups, the insatiable demand for lectures on 'current affairs', politics, economics, sociology, education, psychology, philosophy and religion, and the phenomenal spread of the 'Brains Trust' technique initiated by the BBC have demonstrated in convincing fashion the ardent desire of vast numbers of people

to probe and to master the problems of modern society. (Dent, 1942, p. 72)

From this description of a society reconstructing itself through political discussion of its purposes and plans, Dent took the idea of an active learning role for the child. This learner came from his observations of a citizenry busy reinventing a fairer society, meeting individual and community needs. To join together the individual and the collective, Dent quotes approvingly from a contemporary Ministry of Education pamphlet:

... the approach to learning is made much more by way of activity and experience. (Dent, 1949, p. 84)

To this core idea of the Hadow practical child receiving a curriculum of physical and practical skills is added the role of the practical invention of social skills.

Social training, or more accurately, training in the art of living usefully and happily in community (can be expressed in the junior elementary 7–13 school) ... simple debates and semi-formalised discussions ... (Dent, 1942, p. 58)

In this case the pre-war progressive idea of the developing child, 'learning by doing' was extended into debate and discussion as a way of learning to be democrats, Dent's major aim, the 'educational needs of the democratic community' were a high priority as they were the foundation of the 'good society' he wanted, of which civic responsibility was a key value. A democratic society needed a democratic philosophy of education in which education would have the aim of changing and developing the society, not just reflecting it. In this way, Dent produced an argument for an active education, not just built around the needs of the child but of the demand for a democratic society. Discussion was a key method in the production of the democratic citizen; it joined together a practical pedagogy, a perspective on learning and a social reconstructionist role for the teacher and the learner.

Dent felt that the project method could also help in the social training given by the school. It provided an opportunity for a child to do a piece of work not so much because

he has to as because he wants to play his part in achieving a common purpose. He can be brought to feel, as an individual, his share of responsibility for his own little part of the community. (op. cit., pp. 40–1)

(Although describing the project as investigation, there is no direct mention of discussion here but the argument is congruent with his main thrust.) The reconstructionist school curriculum went beyond the timetable, it involved ethos and an extension of school time. For example, the idea of the school club as a practical forum for civics where the pupil develops as a member of a community was in line with official reports at the time. The Ministry of Education argued in one report that the school club should extend the school community ethos

> by direct means to create a social structure satisfying to the pupil — a structure which he can understand and from which he may learn the discussion of practical difficulties and problems with objectivity and tolerance. (Clubs) provide a powerful means of preventing and combating juvenile delinquency. (Ministry of Education, 1947, p. 16)

Ditto for increasing pupil responsibility in the school, this would

> offer them, if wisely given, an excellent opportunity of learning about the community of which they are members by sharing in its work and organisation. (op. cit., p. 16)

Within the complex discourse of discussion, the reconstructionist school and democracy, there lies contradiction. For example, discussion can appear to mean different things in the wider education argument in which it is contained; sometimes there is an implication that it is a more effective means of inculcating an unchanged body of knowledge and an effective pupil socialization process, at other times it is connected to an argument about an active citizenship and democracy in education and society. These may not be either/or but the discourse works if it offers a comprehensive view which determines action or commitment.

The new secondary modern schools were described by educational commentators as experimental in the sense that direct controls, by the Government and the examining boards, were not exercised and the schools were encouraged to find new ways of teaching. The curriculum was apparently grouped in ways connected by a project method. Harold Loukes, a significant Christian educator and the head of Oxford's Department of Education, described the situation in this way . . .

> . . . these schools had been deliberately unplanned: they were free to develop along their own lines. Local authorities had been encouraged to devise their own schemes. Teachers had been encouraged to experiment with curriculum and method in response to the special needs of their own children. Advice from commissions and from the Ministry of Education had been given in carefully chosen general terms, or if in more detail, by way of illustration rather than precept. The 'plan' for the secondary modern school had been a plan for freedom . . . this meant that the experiments and decisions were to be made by the

men and women engaged in the work itself. In consequence they would be made in a certain measure of isolation. (Loukes, 1956, p. 16)

At the core of the secondary modern experiment was the teacher, given in Loukes' view, unlike the pre-war elementary teacher, a responsibility to devise a new curriculum and pedagogy . . . Within this 'principal of self-determination' for the secondary modern schools, Loukes argued that 'the schools were to be free of central direction, and for a time, of examinations'. This allowed a new method to evolve, the method implicit in the Hadow approach, of meeting the needs of children as they emerged in the day to day running of individual schools. He believed that the

supreme virtue [of the experiment was that] each school [was] free to respond to the actual needs of its own children. (Loukes, 1956, p. 62)

Loukes defined the child in ways that were common at the time viz. practical, unbookish and realistic — interested in the immediate, the adult world or the local area: he quoted Hadow on the 'less academic' curriculum and the concern for the practical and activity. In this he was echoing the received view of the tri-partite classification of the child which the Government advertised. But this led Loukes to an argument about the practical necessity to give these children, the overwhelming majority of schoolchildren, a practical curriculum; included in this was a practical civics or citizenship training.

A new, wide curriculum was created with long lists of subjects, a variety of alternative crafts, projects or centres of interests joining them together, as the teachers saw fit. The teachers then had to deal with a new organizational problem, one they did not have in the old elementaries with their single class teaching,

how far they should be specialists in one or two subjects, or how far they should try to be general class teachers? . . . a broad treatment of their special interests (and then) a grouping of kindred subjects [was Loukes' solution]. (Loukes, 1956, p. 90)

Because Loukes argued that the modern school child needed concrete examples, detail, realistic instances etc, the school was obliged to offer immediate satisfaction and arouse immediate interest in its work or fail. This was in line with the official argument that there were real differences between children and Loukes' description of the 'practical' working class child in the secondary modern schools could be contrasted with descriptions of the abstract thinking of the grammar school child. In Loukes' view, the difference between the grammar schools and the modern school lay in terms of difference in method rather than curriculum (Loukes, 1956, p. 94). Without the incentives and rewards that the grammar school could offer, they had to emphasize 'activity methods and practical work'; they had to dramatize history, make models and experiment in rural science . . . they used debating societies and mock parliaments and councils. He argued that

> If primary education is concerned with the discovery of self and society, then secondary education is the discovery of self in society; it is education for responsibility. (Loukes, 1956, p. 122)

In this way Loukes arrived at the idea of a practical curriculum to create social responsibility: this is the basis for Dent's own view, with something of the same logic.

This was not an uncommon view. A book written a few years before made a similar point

> Young democrats, we know, are not produced through classes of boys and girls sitting at desks and receiving instructions within what may be a tight little aristocracy, but by boys and girls having a fair say in what they shall learn and how they shall set about it . . . It does mean that much more of the work must be decided upon as a result of free discussion. (Dray and Jordan, 1952, p. 21)

The method and the purpose are bound together. The old didactic 'civics' class was to be replaced by an active learning to be citizens in a democracy and topic work, questioning and discussion were to be the democratic pedagogy. In the stages of work of the project method, a particular version of discussion was argued for by its proponents.

> We feel that the principle of joint discussion and joint planning is more stimulating than the carrying out of an imposed syllabus. (Cons and Fletcher, 1938, p. 104)

So, discussion was built into the heart of the method when the pupils used discussion techniques, similar to brainstorming and review, in progressing through the topic. It was suggested that

> Five or six is a useful size for discussion, but two or three is often better for investigation when books or specimens are to be shared. (Dray and Jordan, 1952, p. 83)

Within this new reconstructionist discourse, powerful images are created of the school, the learner and the teacher, these images have shaped the way the post-war period was seen as one of experiment and innovation. Although it was not the purpose of this paper to focus on the contradictions within the discourse, it is clear that the social project was grafted onto the conservative assumptions about the child and its learning present in the legislation (the

1944 Education Act). Yet the move into the social through the idea of responsibility, active citizenship and the invention of a 'practical' pedagogy had resonances and possibilities of action which could not be foreseen at the start or withheld once begun.

How did the opportunities for a new pedagogy emerge in schools? The conditions, according to Dent and Loukes, were considerable. The secondary modern school was new and free from curriculum and examination restraints; its teachers were free to experiment with method. Did a pedagogical shift occur, what was its motive forces and which teachers were involved?

The Pedagogical Shift II

A series of popular books produced by teachers in the late 1950s described, within a semi-fictional narrative convention, the secondary modern schools (Braithwaite, 1959; Blishen, 1955 and 1969; Partridge, 1966; Townshend, 1966). These accounts offer a contrasting way of seeing the changes in the education system. The way teachers see their responsibilities and particularly the way they describe the conditions of their work offer a number of striking counter-images to that offered within the previous discourse yet they also constitute the beginnings of a critique of that discourse and an explanation of the complexities of the reconstitution of teaching work, in relation to change and curriculum history.

Braithwaite (1959) describes a curriculum in his classroom which is practical or based on the pupil's experience. In this classroom, the idea of the practical/social activity, the discussion, is related to active learning, relationships and the wider school.

> We encourage them to speak up for themselves, no matter what the circumstances or the occasion: this may probably take the form of rudeness at first but gradually, through the influences of the various committees and the Student Council, we hope they will learn directness without rudeness, and humility without sycophancy. We try to show them a real relationship between themselves and their work, in preparation for the day when they leave school. (Braithwaite, 1959, p. 32)

> I tried to relate everything academic to familiar things in their lives. Weights were related to foodstuffs and fuel, measurements to dress lengths, linoleum and carpets . . . They eagerly participated, asking me questions with a keenness I had not suspected in them and often the bell for recess, lunch or the end of the day would find us in the heat of some discussion, disinclined to leave off. (Braithwaite, 1959, p. 86)

> Our lessons were very informal, each one a kind of discussion in which I gave them a lead and encouraged them to express their views

against the general background of textbook information. (Braithwaite, 1959, p. 99)

In these extracts, the value of the vision expressed by Dent and Loukes is confirmed. The teacher, through a new technology, of which they are themselves the main aspect, begins to create the realizing mechanism of the new society. The school had become a place to learn through action (and example) the role of the citizen. The moral vision is confirmed in the text.

The accounts given by Blishen (1955 and 1969) are more extensive and complex. An early comment upon the headteacher of the old, worn-out school, goes to the heart of the question about change in this period:

> Why, at the end of his life as a teacher should he try to face the enormous pretence (as it seemed to him) that (school) had been changed by a piece of legislative conjuring into something new and superior? (Blishen, 1955, p. 19)

and continues later in the text with a recognizable vignette of classroom life.

> The tedious orderliness of a class doing its normal work . . . the master orating, or bending over a book, or attacking the blackboard, his mouth opening and shutting with that exaggeration that comes from distrust of one's audience . . . sometimes the teacher would be directing his remarks to one quarter of the room and the rest would have collapsed into freedom. (Blishen, 1955, p. 62)

Written several years into his career in teaching, and ten years after the 1944 Act, the sense of a continuation of older traditions in teaching and classroom work and relations, derived from elementary schools and their teachers, is strong.

In a later book, using recollections, presumably from notes and diaries or written with a sense of the past, Blishen produces a fuller sense of the struggle to create the new direction in pedagogy. Teachers become less heroic and more curmudgeonly than reconstructionist. A description of a colleague, who rejects change, acts as a counterpoint to the author, with his liberal concerns for the pupils and his attempts to teach in a meaningful way.

> Since he regarded the introduction even of geography into the curriculum as a decadent and cynical concession to theorists (and careerists) in Her Majesty's Inspectorate of Schools . . . (he) became apoplectic when the local authority gave us a grant of £15 for an experiment in film appreciation. (Blishen, 1969, p. 96)

His colleague was against films, it was just 'sitting down on bottoms' yet when films were shown everybody found a reason to bring their class. T, his colleague, continues in this vein throughout

Do we have to make them feel their callow opinions are important when most of them can't spell? (Blishen, 1969, p. 246)

How could we invite our boys to give their views on anything whatever? We were there to desperately impose a few simple moral attitudes on them. To solicit opinions was to encourage licence, insolence. (Blishen, 1969, p. 260)

This tension in the staffroom between the attitudes of the older elementary teachers, continuing a culture of work based on subduing a morally deficient working-class, and the demands of the new work in which he is engaged is a sign of the inadequacies of the discourse of social reconstructionism. It was based on a simple idea of the teacher; the teacher had been a slave and now was free; good would ensue.

The labour process of the secondary modern school was based upon servicing a new curriculum but the teachers had different or inadequate skills.

Too many boys had failed to acquire the basic skills in the primary schools, and (the school) . . . had never faced the task of making good. There was too little of the expertise required among the staff, but also too little grasp of the need. (Blishen, 1969, p. 114)

rarely to begin with did we have genuine specialists on the staff; rarely to end with did the incoherent life of the school permit anything like department intercourse between the teachers of any subject. Anyone in the school was likely to be invited to teach almost any subject and the whole organisation hung on syllabuses prepared along the way by our shadowy teachers in charge. Where Mr . . . obtained his history syllabus, no one knew: it proposed the usual trudge through the ages, and the few who really cared (teachers) . . . fretted at this restriction . . . To be positively consulted about any period whatever, let alone to have a whole first year form falling over themselves, to verify their Roman fiction, was more than he had hoped for . . . (Blishen, 1969, p. 115)

This description of the labour process contrasts sharply with the rhetoric of the freed teacher. Social reconstruction and the creation of democracy might be the aims but the means was based upon a culture of work and skill that was unchanged and militated against change. The shift from the role of agent of cultural and social renewal to that of hired labourer, working without skill in rotation, is hard to encompass within a single set of symbols, which the main discourse was attempting. Other reflections on the secondary modern school, written then or later, tended to emphasize the problems of the culture and organization of work. For example, Townsend (1966) in a narrative written more as a warning and less as one of heroic endeavour, reflecting the moral panic of its day, repeatedly stressed the continual changeover of staff in his urban school and the 'battling to survive' condition of the probationer teachers.

In four years, the length of time pupils spent at St. Stephen's, the number of staff who had resigned or insisted on transfer (was) fifty (plus hundreds of temporary teachers). (Townsend, 1966, p. 119)

And

In many London schools, there is a staff turnover of up to 50 per cent each year. Young inexperienced teachers are 'directed' to those schools to cope the best they can; untrained dominion graduates are employed to 'caretake' classes; teaching methods vary from class to class. (Townsend, 1966, p. 131)

With this lack of stability in the new schools, the culture of work was determined even more by the older ex-elementary teachers. Partridge (1966), in a subbiographical description of a school, uses actual conditions to provide a liberal commentary on the state of education and his solutions. Even in the early 1960s, Partridge can describe the culture of work as depending on a headmaster (who)

has brought many of the assumptions of this older tradition (tough Board schools in an industrial area) with him . . . He believes in strictness . . . and that his will must be done. . . . he sees the boys as coming unwillingly to school and as working unwillingly in the classroom. (Partridge, 1966, p. 108)

The culture of work was determined by him and by the older teachers.

There is a general deference to experience and seniority, though not always so. In the course of the dinner time discussions, the stories, jokes and topics of conversation are usually decided by the senior teachers. Seldom does a junior member initiate conversation or voice strong opinions other than or contrary to those of his seniors . . . the essential elements of the status system (age and seniority). (Partridge, 1966, p. 35)

If the young teacher has any liberal or innovative ideas, the culture of work in the school will be against him or her.

. . . he is sure to find classroom teaching an impossibility, and so he has little recourse but to a general whacking session; and the older teachers will nod their heads and say I told you so. (Partridge, 1966, p. 115)

In comparison to the reconstructionist talk of freedom and democracy in the classroom, Partridge describes the classroom as

... just a variety of tasks given them by various teachers, and in which they see little rhyme or reason. (Partridge, 1966, p. 179)

The lack of fit between the way of explaining reconstruction as a movement and an opportunity for teachers, within their new schools and with a new mandate, and the labour process of teaching is enormous. Even sympathetic teachers felt that their identity as new teachers was not in accord with the realities of teachers' work.

Blishen worked hard at the discovery of the technology of discussion, finding his pedagogy through trial and error and not through a grand theorizing about learning and practice. His statements and descriptions about class discussions begins to alter over time; they move from a tentative enquiry

Early in his first year, I was discussing cinema going with his class. What sort of films did we enjoy? ... The general drift of the discussion was that films (i.e. horror films) were good. (Blishen, 1955, p. 79)

through

I let the discussion ramble on until a pattern of opinion had become clear. (Blishen, 1955, p. 149)

The discussion began to collapse. I summed up quickly, sticking scrupulously to the points the class themselves had raised; adding nothing of my own. It seemed for all its inconclusiveness ... a rather impressive review of several of the main issues raised by this sort of writing (Blishen, 1955, p. 151)

until a confidence about practice emerges

At first I had proposed themes for these discussions but in time the class took over there was a rush of very sore subjects close to their hearts; the school leaving age, school dinners, co-education, the prefect system, school rules. (Blishen, 1955, p. 205)

Eventually, the joining of the public and the professional is reached, a discussion method able to work as a technology and as a vehicle for the social/moral reconstruction that the discourse makers and the older teachers were connected to.

There was no difficulty in stimulating discussion of this literature. Most classes provided a fairly wide sweep of views, many of which actually crystallizes during the discussions. I kept my comments to a minimum. I was not needed really as a commentator: I had only to keep the discussion moving. My presence was enough, part of the time; in front of Sir, most of the boys wanted to put their thoughts in some sort of order. Otherwise I had merely to underline a question that needed

> to be answered, a point that ought to be picked up occasionally to hurry down some boisterous siding and bring them back to the main line. The important thing, I became more and more sure as time went on, was to have the talking; to make at least some of them aware, however incompletely and insecurely, that there were matters to be considered, questions to be answered. (Blishen, 1955, p. 152)

The pedagogic shift had occurred in one school at least.

Conclusion

Curriculum history as a field of scholarship has had difficulties discerning classroom practice in the past even though its focus was on the practice of the curriculum. Administrative histories of curriculum associations or exam board minutes are more easily obtained and provide an inferential guide to curriculum practice.

In an early essay on curriculum change, Goodson (1983) argued that the secondary modern schools had a

> . . . freedom (which) allowed many of the schools to experiment with their curricula and to pursue vocational and child-centred objectives. Social studies and civic courses, for instance, were rapidly established in a number of schools. (Goodson, 1983, p. 19)

This comment is in line with those of other commentators on the work of the secondary modern school, some of them reported in this essay. In this period, it is seen as a place of experiment. It is unclear why this should be the case. It was detached from the examination system and, like other kinds of low status work, able to labour in an unsupervised manner. There is an evident truth, in that sense, of how the English education system operates. However, this view implies a correspondence between the public rhetoric of the reconstructionist post-war position and school practice. Because there was said to be freedom and autonomy, there must be freedom and autonomy. The post-war discourse had its own standards and purposes though. While the idea of a new society forging its future in the schools is a powerful one, and one that will have spurred some teachers, it needs examination. Amongst other points to be raised is that of the schools, their resources, work cultures and teachers. Each of these tended to exist at a deeper level than a discourse designed to re-package them for purposes of renewal.

There is some evidence that little was changing in the elementary classrooms. The old elementary schools, their buildings, resources and teaching work cultures dominate the fictional and autobiographical accounts of the secondary modern schools. They did not suddenly disappear. They lived on in the management of the schools, in the work habits of the senior teachers and in the expectations of the children. They continued in the lack of support offered to the new teachers and the high turnover of teachers in the city areas, particularly London. The antipathy to a new curriculum and a new technology of teaching was expressed in the comments about the encouragement of license and insolence and most of all in the inability, in a time of poor resources and little support, to see the child in a different way. The gap between a progressive rhetoric of change in a democracy and the culture and labour process of teachers' work is stark. How could it be otherwise? The surprising point which is not picked up in curriculum history theorizing is that it is not subject associations which define these teachers. Indeed they are generalists, imposed upon by alien subject demands, identifying with a culture of work derived from much older elementary school traditions. These teachers are defined by the pressures of teaching, its reliance on corporal punishment, the seniority system in teaching, the high turnover of urban teachers and the unsupported drift in the newly changing curriculum.

These new teachers are not defined by the nature of the subject and its related career structure as suggested by Goodson (Goodson, 1983, p. 37). Indeed, some of the writers, and perhaps others, are defined in their identities by the claim to a new kind of teaching and a new technology in teaching. Reference to the dominating discourse is not made but the teachers construct their identities, against unfavourable circumstances, in such a way that a new curriculum is forged, a pedagogical shift is made.

If some of the teachers moved to the idea of discussion then where did they get their influences from? Is it possible to construct a new pedagogy by experience and will alone, in a classroom? In what sense can a shift of pedagogy by teachers under these conditions be seen as a development of a systematic body of knowledge upon teaching? What little references can be found to this new way of teaching, which cuts across traditional models of teacher and learner, are nearly all wartime references. Discussion was a necessary invention, created out of adult education practice on the left (Left Book Club not the traditional labour education agencies, such as the National Council of Labour Colleges), pre-war, and, directly or indirectly, linked to the development of army education practice (ABCA). The very idea of discussion as a mass method of education was a wartime phenomenon (see Chapter 5). Who were the agents who could have moved even the minority of teachers into a new pedagogy and one which was the riskiest of all to the teacher? The movement of army personnel into teaching through the emergency-training scheme was associated, in some commentators' minds, with a freshness of outlook, a sense of value in education and a willingness to experiment.

Is a comparison of the philosophical/social text in education and the fiction/autobiographical text valid? Its validity here is partly built upon the point and counterpoint of these sets of information and perspective; the former describes a future which in turn affects teachers and administrators who may or not change. The latter were teachers, writing perhaps for a less idealistic audience, concerned about youth, who consciously tried to write a truth which would counter the image of new schooling embodied in the reconstructionist texts. These were deconstructionist texts, in other words. But the test of the use of these kinds of information for the historian goes beyond the relationships described here. For in what sense can the use of this data sustain the interpretations placed upon them in this essay and their use as a basis for a critique of curriculum history scholarship? In one reading of them, they can't be so used. They could be added to a segmented, chronological description where sources are accumulated, overwhelming the reader with circumstantial evidence. However, the data does not accumulate here, unless the heroic innovator model of the battling teacher is substituted for a more complex picture of ambiguous changes. Yet the data can be used if the purpose is different; proof is exchanged for ambiguity, contrast and layering. In this case, there isn't any proof only possibilities. The area investigated through these sources has allowed a useful contrast to develop between a discourse of change and a practice of struggle and inertia. Both are feasible ways of explaining the period and, together, they produce other possibilities. It isn't a case of either/or but both.

7   A Determining Moment for Teaching: The Strike of 1985

This essay was written in 1985 for the now defunct iconoclastic journal, *Marxism Today*. Teachers in England and Wales were in dispute with their employers at national and local level in the mid-1980s. It was a bitter and protracted dispute and probably as crucial for organized teachers as the miners' strike was later. It was probably one of the last articles written for the journal which took such an orthodox view of struggle and history in the modern period; the journal was already both interpreting and inventing the post-Fordist future. Even when it was produced, this essay did not feel right, it felt out of time and I think it has proved to be so in parts. Yet it was one of the few essays produced about the teachers' strike, in a period which was without doubt a watershed in the political and work relations of education. In a way which the writer could barely have foretold, and which probably confirms the fact I was the wrong choice for *Marxism Today* at the time, the landscape of education was radically changed. This essay was written from within the perspective it was also critical of, that is it assumed that, for example, partnership and professionalism were connected, that they were not just rhetorical flourishes but descriptors of a system and culture as well as being ideological statements about it; a further assumption I held was that space existed within those concepts for alternative meanings and oppositional practices to endure. What I did not understand was that my criticism used the same basic landscape and followed its contours, it was a child of its modern times.

The present teachers' dispute is the most bitter since the war. Underlying it is the changing relationship between teachers and the State. School teachers are in dispute with their employers, the local education authorities, about their annual wage settlement and they have been for over a year. They have been resolute and resourceful in taking various kinds of action and they have grown in confidence and in anger as the strikes have continued. Underlying their action is a strong anxiety about the future of education and, in particular, the plan that Sir Keith Joseph, the Secretary of State for Education, has proposed for the future. The main feature of this plan is the connection made between productivity and pay. Regular assessment of teachers is intended to make them more 'productive' but it will also intensify the controls upon them. The action the teachers are taking and the new structure of work and pay proposed for them are part of a changing relationship between teachers and the central State. The post-war relations have been altered and direct intervention and control of teaching has replaced the old idea of consensus in policy making and management.

The Pay Dispute

Teachers in England and Wales organized in the National Union of Teachers or the National Association of School Masters/Union of Women Teachers, and teachers in Scotland, organized in their own Educational Institute, have been taking action in parallel with each other over the low pay settlement offered to them. Teachers have suffered from a drop in their relative standard of living of about 30 per cent over the last ten years. The Burnham committee, which is similar to Whitley committees in other industries, is the pay negotiating body for the teachers, consisting of their immediate employers, the local authorities, and the various teachers' associations. The employers' panel on Burnham has produced, initially with bad grace, a series of final pay offers, moving the percentage rise from 4 per cent to 6.9 per cent. During the dispute the initiative on the employers' panel has moved from the Conservative dominated county associations to the Labour dominated metropolitan associations which has helped the process of negotiation. However, rate-capping and a Department of Education veto leave little room for flexibility on pay and the last offer, not yet accepted by a majority of the teachers' panel, is dependent on Joseph's assent. He is unwilling to give this as he wants a pay award attached to a change in teachers' conditions of service.

After years of mild paralysis and attrition, caused by a steady erosion in educational spending and a fall in the number of school-age children, the teachers in the NUT and NAS/UWT have organized a pay campaign which has been cathartic in releasing their energy and frustration. Tactics have included withdrawal from lunchtime supervision involving temporary school closure, withdrawal from curriculum and examination development meetings (inside and outside school time), and withdrawal from all the unpaid overtime which teachers undertake for parents' evenings, field trips, evening and weekend sports, in fact anything which is not class teaching. Refusing to teach classes for absent colleagues has also been a useful disruptive tactic. The campaign was initially built around the well-organized branches of the unions, and then, in the NUT's case, by regular balloting of members. It has involved virtually every member of the two unions. The tactics which escalated the action, and which needed firm support and good organization, have been the short day strikes, in blocks of up to three days, and the one hour strikes, sometimes taken by each teacher in turn through the day.

The guerilla campaign, for it certainly is one, has concentrated on local authorities in turn, dividing the employers and then reducing action in the area when the authority supported their case. The NUT recently announced a new

series of targets—the constituencies of government ministers, marginal constituencies, key influential authorities and those authorities which have taken
legal and other sanctions against the union. More schools have begun to close
as headteachers, in an increasingly stressful and isolated position, have been
unable to keep them open.

Joseph has taken action in the Burnham committee to alter the voting on
the teachers' panel by reducing the number of NUT representatives and thereby
seeking to bring the strike to an end. It is not clear at the moment if he will
succeed. A new majority group composed of small headteachers' associations,
a non-striking union plus the NAS/UWT may accept the last final pay offer.
The NUT has remained firm on the question of a large pay award but the other
unions are looking more towards future bargaining on productivity and conditions of service in teaching to increase pay packets. There is some tension
between the NUT and the NAS/UWT on present strategy which is exacerbated
by old rivalries between them. For the first time in a long while the NUT has
taken an initiative on pay and been tenacious and creative in promoting it, and
this has taken the NAS/UWT by surprise and made it unable to use its old cry
of 'sell out' by the larger union. One of the factors in the dispute which has
consistently helped and strengthened the teachers has been the actions of
Keith Joseph. His strategy has failed to finish the strikers with a clear victory
for the Government. His talk of 'improving the teaching profession' has not
been popular with teachers. Many of them feel he is the cause of their dire
financial and educational situation and he has only served to stir them up even
more with his 'improving' rhetoric. At the same time, creating a body of lunchtime supervisors and paying them from future investment for education has
further antagonized teachers.

Pay and Productivity

Much of the energy shown by teachers in the action has been sustained by
their fear of what Joseph intends to do to them and to the education service.
He recently produced a plan, costed at £1.25bn, by which teachers' work and
pay would be closely connected. The plan involves two grades of teachers.
The entry grade, the first three years of teaching, would be an elimination
grade in which regular appraisal would be used to sack 'incompetent' teachers.
The main professional grade would be the other grade and teachers would
get annual pay increments if they pass an annual assessment, and none if
they fail.

There are many relatively young teachers trapped on the bottom two
scales (out of five) of the present pay structure. They are the force behind the
pay dispute. They may also be the teachers who, if the dispute fails, might take
a risk on the merit pay plan as the only other means by which they could get
a decent wage. The risk for them is clear — not everybody is going to pass
the assessments, and it is not yet clear what the criteria for passing would be
nor who would operate the system. More generally the risk is especially clear

for the majority of the teachers, namely the women teachers, who already fail to get promotion and whose average salaries are lower than the men teachers.

The effect of the annual assessment therefore, would be to divide teachers. Moreover it would make them more susceptible to the new supervisory management style of headteaching which Joseph is also promoting. Teachers would have difficulties in organizing in a situation where a number of teachers, determined by local authorities, would get 'extra' pay but others would be made redundant or redeployed elsewhere.

Sir Keith's future plans may go adrift because of an old bogey in teaching. A previous 'merit pay' plan, often called payment by results, operated in teaching up to the late nineteenth century. Teachers were paid according to their examination result in the reading, writing and arithmetic curriculum. Exam cramming, job insecurity and a powerful inspectorate were the result and teachers have not forgotten it. The NUT grew rapidly in response to the teachers' anger and resentment at the system. It is this fear, rather than contemporary parallels with productivity plans in other industries and the disruption they cause to the unity of workers, that is likely to sway the teachers against the plan.

The idea of assessed teacher productivity, coming from Joseph, raises another problem for the main unions, the NUT and the NAS/UWT. The tension between them in the present pay dispute referred to earlier has an historical background which merit pay could intensify. Before 1919 the NUT was the union for qualified teachers but a pay struggle, (not so widespread but more intense than the present one), changed its attitude. It began to operate as an industrial union, recruiting widely, and influenced by syndicalist and guild socialist ideas. Men teachers returning from the war were out of step with the new policy, and annoyed by the gains of the feminists in the union, formed the NAS. They argued for an old craft union policy, but defined not by qualifications but by gender. Their slogans were 'men teachers for boys' and 'the man's family wage'. Over the years this became the career teacher, a phrase which is not far removed from the merit teacher of the new plan. The distance between the unions has revived around the industrial–craft union divide and if Joseph's plan is introduced, it would serve to reinforce this divide. In some areas of the country, notably Birmingham, grassroots unity between the two unions is very high and the Left in the NUT, the Socialist Teachers' Alliance, is presently arguing for a merger between them. But there is also the possibility that they may divide further over the benefits to be gained from a productivity deal and this would be disastrous for any further campaigns on pay or any other issue.

Teachers and the State

The strength of the pay action and the productivity proposals from the Government are both signs that the relationship between teachers and the State is changing.

Since the last war, partnership has been the key word in any description of the relations between teachers, the local authorities and central government. Teachers were partners in the process of educational policy-making in joint bodies, such as the Schools Council for the Curriculum, and in numerous other important agencies, such as the school examination committees. Regular meetings, both formal and informal, were held between union leaders (especially the leaders of the NUT) and ministers and DES officials.

Today, teachers don't see partnership but control as the main feature of the education service. The Schools Council was abolished and the NUT is now excluded from many of its old places of influence and consequently unable to negotiate in the old way anymore.

Decision-making in education now comes from the Department of Industry as well as the DES, and a major new capital equipment and curriculum initiative in secondary schools comes from the Manpower Services Commission. Cost accountants, like Price Waterhouse, now work in schools and with privatization of schoolcleaning about to happen, Pritchards (the cleaning contractors) will follow.

Teachers feel cornered. The very idea of being a teacher is under threat. The school curriculum depends more and more on parental fund-raising, staff are compulsorily redeployed to other schools, a permanent contract is a rarity among younger teachers and so on. Being a teacher always involves some idea of change and improvement and this is impossible to sustain in a service which is being systematically contracted. Teachers cannot teach for unemployment, and they are doing just that for the majority in many parts of the country. There is a moral crisis about the gap between what they think teaching and education is and what they feel it is becoming.

Control has replaced partnership, or at least it looks like that to many. Joseph has taken to himself sweeping powers of control over, and intervenes directly in, the education service and this appears to the post-war generation of teachers and their union leadership as something akin to dictatorship. In fact, Joseph is reasserting the traditional role of the State in the educational system and reverting to the direct management that was common at the turn of the century. What is odd is that he is acting under the 1944 Act, an Act which several of his predecessors at the DES explained made them unable to act! The partnership mythology was built around an Act which is now being used to shift power back to the central State.

The parallels between the situation in the 1920s and today are striking, but the choices made by Joseph's Tory predecessors are directly opposed to his own. He has taken powers — disused or latent — that were available to him to intervene in, and alter, the system in a direction he favours. In doing so he risks exposing the power relations in the system (previously said to be equal — a partnership) and radicalizing teachers. In Stanley Baldwin's administration in the 1920s, Lord Eustace Percy had a similar post to Joseph's. He used his powers to set up a system of 'indirect rule', borrowed from the colonies, where a 'relative autonomy' was given to the 'natives', thereby rejecting oaths of allegiance to the State and a more heavily controlled teaching force along the lines of the civil service. He did this for several reasons, all of which may be overturned by the present Government. Percy wished to deregulate the system and allow the local authorities to be a buffer between the teachers and the central State. He thereby removed himself from daily control while retaining overall strategic control. Joseph on the other hand is seeking to reduce the role of local authorities to that of agents and supervisors.

If partnership is to be written off and direct control reasserted, then its likely consequence, if the past history of the NUT is anything to go by, is a more radicalized, better-organized union. However, if merit pay is introduced, this could be in the context of a more splintered profession.

The Future of Teaching

Some things will never be the same again after this pay struggle. Certainly the dispute will have created a new sense of togetherness amongst many teachers. What happens to relations between NUT and NAS/UWT members will probably depend on the outcome of the dispute. The headteachers are being forced away from the teachers to become 'managers', and in the near future may even be recruited from outside teaching. Teachers' voluntary duties may cease to exist in some schools after the teachers' present sanctions. In other schools they may become the most bearable part of teaching and so continue.

Relations with parents seem to have varied during the dispute. There has been good overall support but no doubt even sympathetic parents have become exasperated with the guerilla tactics. Soon parents will occupy half the school governing bodies. Unless teachers can make political allies of them, engaging in joint campaigns for school resources or on local authority policies, then schools will be occupied in arguments between parent and teacher.

Women teachers in primary schools are the basis of the NUT's strength and their determination in this dispute may lead to better representation in the union's leadership and may even transform its internal politics and ways of working. The feminization of the workforce took place at the turn of the century but only at critical moments has it been followed by the temporary feminization of the union. There is no longer a need to use married women teachers as a labour reserve to be employed at will, specially as part-timers. That, and the pressure of women's changing expectations, mean that attention will increasingly focus on policies for equal opportunity. Local equal opportunity committees in the union in fact have already become significant agents for change in the local branches.

A change for the better which has taken place in the last few months is in the relations between the NUT and the Educational Institute of Scotland. The Scottish teachers have been striking longer and they are now taking the final sanction at the workplace — refusing to participate in the 1986 school examinations. They have caused chaos in Scotland, a much more centralized system of educational government than England and Wales, by withdrawing from curriculum development and the introduction of a new secondary examination. One of the reasons for the greater unity in the pay dispute in Scotland is that it has been a deliberate union policy not to allow the development of different pay grades, making it easier to get support for a straight percentage rise.

There seems to be no drift to Labour although it retains support in the metropolitan areas and teachers have a high profile in urban constituency parties. What could Labour offer teachers? Labour's present ambiguous claim to increased educational expenditure might be attractive but is insufficient. New ideas about public service in a state system or a revamped equality of opportunity seem unlikely. Labour may inherit a clearly centralized system of education and this would make it at odds with its teachers. Perhaps a new alliance between teachers and Labour for educational advance may not be forthcoming. If this is so, then the teachers' next step will be to make the union a source of alternative policies in education formed in resistance to central state policy, and to forge local and national alliances to promote them.

Conclusion

From the perspective of England in the 1990s it is a different time as much as the educational inquiries of the TLL in the 1920s and the spirit of social renewal in the 1940s. It marks the end of a period when organized teachers were able to work through and influence state agencies and government servants by right through joint committees, pressure group politics and fraternal relations. Soon after the dispute came the radical reorganization of education in which a statutory national and testing framework curriculum emerged, collective bargaining was abolished, teacher salaries were lodged within the school budget and school governing bodies framed new employment policies within national contracts for teachers. Surface features of the old system began to disappear including reference to the English system of education as a partnership between teachers, local and national government. Professionalism began to lose its hegemonic significance as the employers, union leaders and ministry servants found its explanatory value drift away from the new realities of the state system and its teachers' responsibilities and duties.

The essay has some value though. It marked the end of collective bargaining as the Burnham Committee was abolished soon afterwards along with the annual pay round. This was not just a minor, technical procedure or even the end of a period of industrial rights for teachers; it represented the end of a defining period of modernity in education as Burnham symbolized the entry, in the early 1920s, of teachers into a central government domain as one of the first groups of public servants to be treated as a significant group of state employees. It was this act, as well as the new education act of 1919, which began the early modern discourse of professionalism and partnership. The abolition of Burnham symbolizes the end of this period.

Surprisingly, for a person unable to extrapolate clearly from the present to the future, there are some points which still make sense. It was seen then, and can still be seen, as a crucial time in the relations between teachers and the State. Increased centralization, rising privatization and the rise of managerialism were discerned clearly. The continuing problem for the State of strategic and operational control was raised but not the attempted solution of local quasi-markets and mandatory work (in curriculum and assessment) nor the enforced decline of the local authorities in education.

Some indications of the threatened productivity and efficiency drive never really came and appraisal was one of them or at least it appeared in a form which was not threatening but developmental. Union mergers were a non-starter. The need to recruit to survive, the shrinking teaching force and its rapid turnover continues to make unions emphasize either their difference from each other or their services. The ability of the health service, local and civil service unions to merge in the 1990s should not be taken as any guide to the actions of the teacher unions. The emergence of women, especially in the NUT, was to be seen in the 1980s disputes but the optimism in the essay was based on this period and not the actual conditions of work for women in teaching, the overall decline of members attending union meetings continues. Certainly the NUT established an Equal Opportunities department, later merging it with Education.

In two major ways, the essay got it wrong and only shows its presuppositions and implicit reasoning in retrospect. As the pillars of modernism, the unions, declined in membership and searched for effectiveness in the decentralization and local, fragmented features of education, their national role was obliterated. Commenting on the sidelines seems a barely adequate response yet the only possible one at the time and later. External signs of radical but better organized teacher unions are not visible although a decentralization of union structures, with a shift of resources nearer to the local areas is; so is the selling of the union through the services it offers, such as cheap car loans and insurance. Only the teachers' boycott of assessment in the late 1980s showed how the unions might be able to work together, and with their members, within a system which refused to recognize them. The success of the boycott points to a low key but very effective form of action now available to teachers who work in a decentralized and exclusionary system. The second error was the older sense in which Labour was seen as the natural home for teachers and one which had spoken most freely in times past of professionalism and partnership. But Labour spent many more years in the wilderness where it could not afford to be seen to be attached to the labour unions, particularly the teacher unions, and could not explain how it would re-establish trust and negotiations, if not a partnership, with teachers. Indeed as the conservative reforms took hold, and interference with them would only increase the teacher's workload again and as it became clear that Labour would be unlikely to alter the overall effects of the reforms, the idea of an 'auld alliance' based on past relations looked threadbare as an idea. If Labour gets teachers' votes, they will probably do so because they are not conservative. More so, they will probably get their vote for reasons to do with the economy or social policy and not educational policy, and perhaps they always did.

8 Reform Dilemmas for the Union: Cultural Change and the Labour Process

Reform and the Unions

The relations between teacher unions and school reform has been raised by the school restructuring shift in the USA and especially by the pivotal role the unions are being asked to play within some appeals for change. This contrasts with the relative silence about teacher unions and school reform in England. However, the paper uses this contrast to raise questions about how the idea of the union is defined and the boundaries around it viewed. The union is often seen as a tightly contained unit, operating as a discrete entity and remaining consistent over time. I will be arguing here that it is a site of production as well as of distribution and that in the modern period it acted as a place where ideas about the work of teachers, its sites and organization, as well as the purpose and form of education were created and circulated. Unions, seen within this frame of reference, were able to act as reform aware places but they have to cope with a major contradiction in this task. Teachers' work, the heart of the union's purpose, might be improved, downgraded or even made redundant by the reform proposals, it may be sought to alleviate or solve a problem of the labour process it contains. Either way, engaging in reform talk is both a necessary and a disruptive act within the union. Another way in which this might be seen is that either stalling or proposing reform will lead to the improvement of or a regression in teachers' conditions of work. For those who win, there are those who will lose. They will be in the wrong sector or with the wrong qualifications.

Reform

School restructuring in the USA has involved teacher unions in different cities, such as Cincinnati, Rochester and Chicago. Reforming schools in England has not involved teacher unions at all.[1] What does 'involved' mean? In a growing US literature, schools can only be reformed if teachers take responsibility for pupil learning and progress, and through their unions develop a partnership with school boards, managers and parents to extend and deepen the reforms. In doing so the teachers would be entering a contract with the community in which their professional responsibilities would be increased and their security and remuneration stabilized. Involved means more than this though. There is an assumption made that teachers and their unions were not involved in taking responsibility for teaching and learning. Commentators have explained this by reference to the collective bargaining system which reduced progress to a yearly set piece battle and reduced questions of responsibility to that of the manager's right to impose and the teacher's right to oppose. Others refer to the effects of the election system in the local school boards and the degree of teacher surveillance and control it created in many smaller districts and also to the history of limiting the responsibilities and power of the teacher in the US through the centralized system of curriculum creation and teacher proofing in the period of extensive centre/periphery model use. A paradox provided in the comparison between the US and England is that the dominant explanation for the role of the teacher in England for many years (and especially the post-war years) is that the teacher was responsible for the curriculum and the pedagogy in the school through a partnership with the local and central state via the teacher unions. Yet it is this discourse which was interrupted by the conservative reforms of education in the late 1980s so severely that it was the union and the teacher who were deliberately excluded from the reforms. They were excluded from the deliberations about the reforms, the pace of their introduction and discussion about their operation and review. The success of the reforms was to be judged by other criteria than whether teachers took an enhanced responsibility for their success. In the first instance teachers were instructed to operate them (down to the hours spent on parts of the curriculum, the forms of testing required and later on the pedagogy suitable) although without the commitment of many teachers they could not have been made operational.

The idea of being involved in, or excluded from, reform through the ways in which the language of reform is used and the silences within it is a useful starting point for this essay. While professionalism is spread around at times of reform or within explanations of system operation, it is constantly being redefined and its meaning is deeply contextualized within the field of reform or system explanation it is being used in. In the 1920s, a new language of professionalism emerged which emphasized the qualities, responsibilities and social role of the teacher at the same time as the education system was being restructured and its purpose and operational control was being challenged by the teacher. A particular and dominant way of regarding and constructing the teacher was reworked (but not really altered) which was suited to the purpose of managing teachers, representing the democratic system of education in England and describing the structural roles of the education system. This worked as a discourse most effectively when the system was not in stress or being challenged. It could be used to discipline, isolate and encourage teachers effectively but alternative strategies were needed when radical change was needed. A sign of its lack of use value came in the mid 1980s when a new system of education was being produced and a new language of competency began to replace responsibility as a key descriptor of teacher quality. By the extended strikes of the mid 1980s in England the Minister of Education was unable to use the term at all in drawing back teachers from the brink and re-establishing control over them. Not until a managerial recast of the reforms, produced because of teacher and system overload in the early 1990s, did the term re-emerge effectively as a new kind of tightly focused responsibility, and this was probably due to the influence of human resource management, rather than New Right ideas on professional monopolies, on the manager concerned, Dearing.

Like professionalism, reform is not neutral or fixed in its meaning. Indeed, as an explanatory idea, it is value-laden before it enters the field it is intended to explain. It implies that the course of action is the required improvement and the necessary corrective. In its usage certain courses of action become legitimated or authorized, and others excluded or silenced.

It is a term that can have no constant meaning, being different in different places and different times. What is often consistent though is the absence of historical context in the argument for reform and the restrictions in the case for reform which do not allow for complexity and distance. A simple political statement is used to generate policies which try to harness forces for change but at the expense of cultural strategies or anything other than system-based analyses. Reform movements may have to give the impression of internal consistency but they appear to represent different constituencies in temporary alliance. Certainly the radical reforms of the Conservative Government in England in the late 1980s used simple ideas of the market or parental power to harness often contradictory tendencies present in their ranks; these included a return to selective education, the expansion of private education, the restoration of conservative values in the curriculum and school life, the modernization of the youth training programme and an expansion of vocational programmes in schools. A tension between restorationist and modernizing tendencies was barely managed and leaked out at different times. David Tyack's description of US restructuring 'as a synonym for the market mechanism of choice, or teacher professionalisation and empowerment, or decentralisation and school site management etc.' (Tyack, 1990) is probably a reflection of the confusion of objectives in many reform movements. Reform policies can try to legitimate their actions by reference to an economic crisis or moral panic and they usually reside within an alliance of management and political parties.

Within this mobilizing of action and the privileging of terms and definitions, reformers assume that the union is implicated and often as an opponent. If reform is dynamic then the union is static; reform is radical and the union will be conservative. In this simple engineering model the union is viewed as a force which may block or destabilize the action. The greater the emphasis placed on the reform the more the union has to be harnessed for change or bypassed. But this model excludes the possibility that the union is not a simple unit of energy, it is a site of production. It can create its own effects and is itself dynamic though disciplined by the need to seek advantage for its members and by its responsive functions. I am using reform to mean, from the union's view, a perspective upon the system in which the teacher and the union reside and an active role in shaping that system which may be licenced by an ambiguous but dominant legitimating discourse.

From the viewpoint of the mid-1990s, it appears perverse to argue that teacher unions have a role in policy but the dominating discourse since the 1920s, and certainly since the late 1940s, is that teachers, through their unions, were partners in the education service. It has been argued that this was a form of indirect control over the teachers but it is also a space in which to move. It is certainly the case that teachers were often seen as meddling in politics and reform by their employers, implying that they were employees without rights on the direction and purpose of the education service. They were to be reformed not to be reformers.

Early research literature on the main post-war union, (the NUT) tended to concentrate on the campaigns or politicking it engaged in to affect policy changes in education. As a variant on systems thinking, the structuralist approaches of Tropp and Manzer view the union as a discrete entity, operating as a single unit, and working through its coherent policy goals in public and private arenas. Manzer described the pay campaigns of the 1960s as not directed at the public to influence the Government, the classic tactic of pressure group politicking, but to create a favourable environment from which to strengthen its regular channels of influence, by consultation and negotiation, with the Government (Manzer, 1970). Tropp argued that these campaigns were part of a search for alliances to further the aims of the union and that they were aimed at any group capable of aiding the union. Union campaigns are not so common they can be overlooked but it is not clear the basis upon which they should be judged. Are they only an adjunct of the main policy negotiation and are they a utilitarian means of seeking support from other social groups? This approach appears to suggest that the public campaign is only a tactical expression of union policy goals which are likely to relate to pay and conditions. Politics appears as a question of corridors and 'men in suits', not as a process of enquiry into the mobilization of members and the public to achieve common goals in public policy and to overcome severe internal difficulties. This is not only a reflection on the received view of internal politics in the union but a very limited view of the external relations and alliances of the union.

Unions are internally dynamic and can create and sustain an identity by their search for an effective means of resisting the controlling version of the teacher represented in the union. It is this identity, epitomized in an official version of the teacher, which places the union clearly within the education service and helps it to recruit. At least this was the case with the National Union of Schoolmasters which was founded in the male-dominated boys' elementary schools in the 1920s (especially the Catholic school of the North West) in opposition to the National Union of teachers and its perceived dominance by women teachers (not just numerically but in policies and even image). To sustain itself, it worked against its rival by attacking the Burnham agreements on pay structure and awards as working to the detriment of the male teacher. Working within its time, it began with a revised craft labour perspective, building it upon the idea of an elite of teachers defined not by their skill but by their sex. Men teachers deserved more pay to increase their numbers by making teaching more attractive and because their role as bread-winners made it necessary. As they could not achieve this end by force nor by alliances, they tried to invent educational arguments which could be used to win advantage with the Government and against the other union. The idea of 'men teachers for boys' did just that. It sought to reform the education of elementary children by explaining that perversion and criminality was the direct result of boys not having male role models in their teachers and as a secondary argument, that women should be raising families and not be in paid labour. The boundaries between the two unions and the way they were then maintained and acted upon, in arguing for or against reforms in education, was determined by this use of symbols and representations. Until they could no longer be sustained because of shifts in work or a new policy context, the NAS always tried to intervene in reform periods by trying to shape the images of the debate around issues of gender, social control and deviancy. By the 1990s its iconography was becoming more complex and guarded appeals to 'career' teachers were overlaid on the older, masculinist symbols.

Unions also have a positive but complex relation to reform which this paper will try to illustrate from the English and Welsh experience of the comprehensive school reform movement in the 1950s, 1960s and 1970s by *firstly* exploring the way in which a new culture of teachers is created and flourishes in and out of the union with reform as its *raison d'être.* I would like to develop a description of how the internal and external aspects of·union policy are linked by the involvement of teachers who are shaped and influenced by the period in which they are working and in turn influence and organize the union. In this way the question of school reform and the union has to be seen over time, related to generations of activists and a policy discourse which saw teachers as legitimate partners in change. The union was most active in reform movements in periods when there was a strong political will in the society for change or as it tried to defend reforms in periods of anti-egalitarian reaction. Therefore the union was most active for reform during and after the two world wars. *Secondly,* by recording the dilemmas of the union when promoting a reform of schooling when the labour process in teaching is to be changed by it. Reforms change conditions of work. Some teachers benefit, others may not. Both groups of teachers may be within the same union or may belong to different unions. A reform is not neutral to a union membership, to be decided by whether the reform idea is itself attractive or not; it will affect their work. This goes beyond questions of site or management or size. At the heart of the representation of the school reform there is usually a prospect of a child and its education; this is not a neutral idea for the teacher, based in different kinds of schools and in different areas. The teacher's own technology, trained and devised for a different kind of child might be treated as outmoded or worse the teacher might be treated as redundant.

Reforming Secondary Education: The Union As a Site of Production of Policy

The National Union of Teachers recruited its members from the elementary schools, the state schools provided locally for the working class: it did not recruit from the secondary schools which were few in number and for relatively few middle class children. Initially, the union supported a reform of the divided system — Beatrice Webb, the Fabian socialist, described union policy, in 1915, as

> an all-embracing system of public education from the infant school to the modernised university, administered by one elected local authority, regulated by one central government department, and served by a homogeneous body of salaried men and women, disciplined by one type of training and belonging to one professional organisation. (Webb, 1915)

In this vision of a coherent education service the union was well in advance of the central government and many local education authorities. During most of the early decades of the century the union supported small-scale additions to secondary education which extended it to other children even though the main class division intact would be preserved. It supported official reports which proposed a universal system of post-primary education even though this education would have promoted further internal divisions, separating children into different kinds (central, senior and technical). The union, pre-war, was moving slowly towards experimental post-primary schools, trying to encourage local authorities to create 'multiple bias schools'. In 1930, a group linked to the union by many joint members, the National Association of Labour Teachers, called for experiments with single site 'multilateral schools' joining different type schools together and this time including the privileged secondary schools (NUT, 1929; NALT, 1930). Their policy was to

> favour a system under which all children of a given area would attend the same secondary school, finding within it varying courses to suit their individual needs, but doing much work in common and enjoying a common social life within the school. (NUT, 1929, p. 2)

By 1935, the NUT was asking for a common secondary school where local conditions allowed (NUT, 1935). The idea of a multilateral school became the means and the end for a common secondary school; for some within the union (and its allies) it was a goal, for others it was a way station. The Labour Party, by 1939, tried for an internal party compromise on education policy and suggested local authorities should build purpose-built common schools in new development areas (Barker, 1972). Because of the competing interests and sectionalism in the union, national union policy was described so . . .

> no firm stand was taken at any time . . . and . . . maximum internal flexibility was preserved. (Fenwick, 1976)

Gradually, as more teachers moved into these new comprehensive schools and lost their allegiances to the old divided schools, NUT policy was able to change.[2] By 1969, a resolution at the annual conference called on the education minister to

> actively intervene forth with and demand that local education authorities present comprehensive schemes of secondary reorganisation immediately. (Benn and Simon, 1970)

So, the consistent support for the state system had gradually developed into a policy for secondary education, based on different sectors for different types of children, and then into a policy of active promotion of the common secondary school reform. How had this happened, who had promoted this policy in the union and what obstacles had been overcome?

Naturally reform movements in society often involved teachers as individuals, and in the English context for most of the century, this has meant an equality of opportunity project, usually supported from a broad left within the union, connected to the Labour Party and to a lesser but significantly qualitative degree, the Communist Party. The reform of education always took second place to the achievement of decent salaries and the protection of its members but the union expressed concern for the quality of state education consistently within its conferences, publications and alliances. By the 1930s, union policy was moving toward a single site purpose-built school policy for the post-primary age range and by 1969, it was supporting comprehensive education as union policy. Who was moving the union in the direction of change? A core of teachers, radicalized by the first war and the salary disputes (Lawn, 1987a), had moved into a loose, left, cross-union group, the Teacher's Labour League, in the 1920s. Small in number, they were still part of the reforming tide in the labour movement. Their main preoccupation was with reactionary local employers but their magazine, the *Educational Worker*, produced articles on new kinds of schooling and members visited Dora and Bertrand Russell's School, A.S. Neill's Summerhill and the progressive Bedales, later even going to the Soviet Union. They discussed pedagogy and teaching style, deliberating on a class-conscious education and bias in textbooks. They became embroiled in inter-party politics and split: a Labour Party affiliate, the National Association of Labour Teachers, was one result. NALT's prologue to their important document, *Education: A Policy*, described its membership as

... all members of the Labour Party, and thus particularly well qualified to deal with educational problems from the professional and the
social point of view. Their object is to assist the authorities in drawing
up an educational programme and to bring that programme, and the
policy underlying it, to the notice of the world outside. (NALT, 1930,
p. 1)

The NUT was the largest union and the debates in the Labour movement
were to influence and in turn be influenced by teachers who were involved
in both arenas. Prominent Labour politicians were ex-schoolteachers and
prominent Labour activists were leading members of the NUT. However the
interlinking of a social reform and educational reform movement within teaching took place at a deeper level than a mixing of a labour leadership elite. In
union associations, particularly in London, activists from the 1920s and 1930s
re-emerged during and after the last war as key members: leaders of the grammar school section (a key player in reform), such as Sam Fisher or of south
London teachers, such as Nan Macmillan.[3] Evidence for the existence of these
teachers in union networks is not as easily gathered as the evidence for the
actions of executive members, through minutes or biographies but their role
in reform can be deduced from their presence at meetings or in publications.
The continual pressure at committee meetings and at the annual conference
from the left, particularly in the grammar school section led to change.

Reforming the Labour Process

A second aspect of school reform with which the union found some difficulty
was producing a coherent policy faced with divided members. Comprehensive
school reform was an example of the complex or ambiguous response which
the union produced to face the external world while trying to resolve or overcome internal contradictions. These contradictions are drawn from the fact
that teachers were employed in the schools which would be replaced, that
there was a significant group in favour of the selective entry schools (grammar
schools) and the idea of a common school pupil was in apparent conflict with
the reality of different schooling for different children. Further complications
were created by the need for the union to protect itself and its recruitment *vis
à vis* other smaller unions; a false or unpopular move internally would ant-
agonize the grammar teachers' union and allow a sectarian (men teachers)
union to recruit. A reform is not neutral and a union must respond to it not
just on its own merits but on its effect on the cohesion and growth of the
union. This may appear opportunistic to the outsider but it is based on the
same organizational imperatives as other kinds of work.

A discussion about the sectionalism in the union, post-war, describes the
policy towards a comprehensive school reform as one of 'maximum internal
flexibility'. This compares with a grammar teachers' union response described

as having 'consistently over-reached themselves in their opposition to the comprehensives' and the men teachers' union response described as one of 'sceptical neutrality' (Fenwick, 1976, p. 151). The rather independent London association of the NUT pushed hard for a London plan while the NAS was sceptical. The union debates were between the pro-comprehensive lobby and those who were trying to retain consensus. Both were satisfied by the undertaking of further research for their own separate reasons. Response is then, in part, tactical. Closer examination of the union response reveals a further contradiction in reform, the labour process for many teachers is affected. While the elementary teachers may be persuaded by the benefits of a recognized common secondary school, including a higher status curriculum and examination and an improved professional training, their erstwhile colleagues in the selective grammar schools were more concerned with a loss of benefit. Their schools had already lost some of their autonomy in the post-war reorganization and were controlled by local education authorities; they had their terms lengthened and had lost holidays. A council meeting declared their resolute opposition to all forms of restrictive regulation in the guise of educational reform (Gosden, 1972, p. 345). Writing in the 1950s, a researcher argued that teachers were against the reform because of the likely size of the resulting schools. Among the problems were 'new problems of organization and human relations', such as a non-teaching headteacher/administrator, the variety of new specialized posts and the reservation of senior posts by the ex-grammar teachers (Tropp, 1957, p. 261). The size of the experimental schools worried some teachers. They appeared to involve new levels of bureaucracy (curriculum directors, counsellors, deputies and administrators) and rising levels of non-teaching staff (librarians, laboratory technicians, audio-visual assistants, clerks and ground staff). Yet training for staff to manage these large institutions was inadequate. There were more departments, sections and units to which teachers belonged and each of them needed regular meetings to function efficiently (Benn and Simon, 1970, pp. 347–66). No wonder that it took until 1965 for a joint meeting of the grammar, comprehensive, secondary modern and technical sections of the union to pass a resolution at conference calling for an overall comprehensive system and that this was an achievement based on years of lobbying, research and debate in the union (Fisher, 1992).

The Union and School Reform: The Case Reviewed

In this paper I have drawn two problems associated with the union and school reform from the case of the long move toward comprehensivization in England. Firstly, school reform was part of a continuing reformist wave in the wider society, a social movement which encompassed the teachers, the union and political parties. The union cannot be treated in isolation from this movement. Alain Touraine identified social movements as

> . . . the organised collective behavior of a class actor struggling against his [sic] class adversary for the social control of historicity in a concrete community. (Touraine, 1981)

The identity of the social movement went deeper than its surface tensions and into, amongst other things, the fight for a new kind of education which coalesced around the idea of comprehensivization.[4] Beginning in and outside the union in the 1920s, in the Teachers' Labour League and later the National Association of Labour Teachers as well, in the Communist Party, the Labour Party and other political groups, the movement took off after the war when its focus on the creation of a new common school system went with the grain of social reform, grounded on the shift to equality of opportunity and the adoption of the union as a corporatist agency (in partnership with central and local government). The union became the major link between individuals and groups and acted as an effective way of exerting pressure publically and mobilizing support.

Secondly, the union has to deal with members who will lose out as well as those who will gain, in a situation where members, and therefore effectiveness as a union, may well be lost. The union is a broad church and a reform affects the labour process, and its underlying rationale (in teaching, ideas on learning and pedagogy, classroom organization, support structures etc), in ways which a defensive organization finds difficult to do more than resist or try to avoid. New jobs are created and old ones lost: this is not just a technical but a human problem. It should be recognized that education is work and school reform is like changing the production line or redesigning the office, it has consequences for a union which go beyond whether it sounds like a good idea or not.

Notes

1 This essay grew out of an AERA panel, reviewing Kerchner and Mitchell's 'idea of a Teacher Unionism' and a Birmingham research seminar based on it.

2 In 1950, there were only ten comprehensive schools in England and Wales; in 1958, there were forty-six and in 1960, there were 130.

3 The extensive evidence of networks of teachers in organized parties and movements (such as the Left Book Club) *and* the union exists within a continuing set of life histories I am developing based in the 1920s to the 1950s. This is not an argument about numbers so much as purpose and intensive endeavour on the part of a few.

4 This view of union internal struggle I take to be distinct from the utilitarian use of contrastive argument for the purpose of factional gain (as described by Kerchner and Mitchell) although it may have some outward similarities.

9 The End of the Modern in Teaching?: Implications for Professionalism and Work

It is the argument within this collection of essays that a major period in the development of teaching, its professionalism and work processes, might be coming to an end in England. It was a period in which a modern system of education was established by a social democratic movement within a particular cultural and organizational framework defined by its 'Englishness'. This period came into being in the immediate post-war, built on the foundations of work in the 1920s and 1930s, established itself in the 1940s , 1950s and 1960s, and began to receive a number of severe shocks in the 1970s. Within this period, especially after the Second World War, the education service was often described as a collective partnership between local and national government and teachers. This idea of partnership was in part mythological, built around the idea of a peculiar 'Englishness', a post-war myth about real English democracy as opposed to continental dictatorships, and it involved a permitted decentralization of the system in which the appearance of autonomy disguised a form of 'indirect rule' from the centre. In this period of 'autonomy and partnership', the involvement of teachers in the governance of education was described as professionalism; this was seen by contemporary observers as a right as well as a responsibility (for example, Tropp, 1957). In recent years, especially since the 1980s and the Thatcherite turning over of education in the 1988 Education Reform Act (and subsequent legislation), the myths and mock traditions of the partnership have been exposed. One consequence of the restructuring of teachers' work (post-ERA emphasis on performance and productivity in a market) is the redesignation of the idea of teacher professionalism and the relationship between that idea and the labour process of teaching.[1]

In this chapter, I want to draw attention to the contradictory nature of the relation between teachers and the rise of modern work in the post-war period, in particular the way in which the progressive social and education policies many teachers supported, delivered a labour process which controlled and tried to determine them. This labour process owed a lot to the contemporary shift towards 'Fordist' methods of production and the employers' way of managing teachers.[2] However, post-war modernism may also be seen as a continuation of a project to incorporate public sector professionals, including teachers, into the welfare functions of the State, not just a method of production. Underlying this essay is an interest in the way in which teachers, no longer able to bargain collectively and with no semblance of a joint project for a fairer society with a corporatist state, may make some gains at school level in a quasi-market but will have lost a sense of progress and the organizing myths that went with it. In this paper, I look firstly at the association of particular kinds of labour processes with the post-war rise of modern schooling and secondly, try and discern the implications for teachers of the new labour processes emerging after the 1988 Education Reform Act.

The Modern Teacher

The post-war period in the education system is the key period in the definition of the modern teacher however its roots lay in the developing social democratic idea of the teacher, the education system and the State, beginning around the First World War, which is one of the main influences on the idea of a public service, post-Second World War. For example, Sydney Webb, the Fabian thinker, described the relation between a new government function of a 'systematic education', the large number and special knowledge of teachers and their claim to

> exercise a professional judgement, to formulate distinctive opinions upon its own and cognate services, and to enjoy its own appropriate share in the corporate government of its working life. (Webb, 1918, p. 3)

It is this description of the teachers taking 'an increased measure of corporate responsibility' for the running of the service (partly to mitigate a state bureaucracy) which has a striking resonance in the post-war period (the 1940s and 1950s). Webb was arguing for the co-optation by the State of a large and growing group of workers who had to be turned away from working for the rich and powerful and towards 'the entire community' viz.

> . . . it is the duty of each profession to take the needs of the whole community for its sphere . . . it must claim as its function the provision of its distinctive service wherever this is required, irrespective of the affluence or status of the persons in need . . . it must emphatically not regard itself as hired for the service only of those who pay fees and it must insist therefore on being accorded by public authority and where necessary at the public expense, the opportunity and the organisation that will enable this full professional service being rendered wherever it is required. (Webb, 1918, p. 8)

Teachers had to serve everybody and be given the means to do this. Webb went on to propose that the Teachers' Registration Council became a Standing Advisory Council to the Ministry of Education and that every local education authority (managing the education service in the localities and regions) be statutorily required to appoint a local advisory committee, representative of all grades of teachers to be nominated by the local professional associations.

Webb's contribution lies in his thinking about the nature of the corporatist structure of the modern state, yet other factors described elsewhere also helped shape this state in practice, not least of which was the post-war arrival of the Labour Government, the urgent need to rebuild the schools (with a scarcity of resources), the implementation of a new education system (following the 1944 Act) and the shortage of teachers. Most of all perhaps was the creation of the welfare system, which incorporated education within the distribution of benefits, following the success of the schools as agents of welfare in the preceding wartime. It is this association with the emerging welfare services which probably affected teachers' work the most, not only with its prevailing sense of public service (now consolidated into this welfare version) and new pedagogical styles (a pastoral child-centredness etc.), but in the nature of its labour process. For example, it has been argued that

> We built public services on the assumption of certainty for a world in which the problems faced were known and the challenges clear . . . so we built services on a uniform basis, limiting choice, and we built an enclosed organisation that limited public access and public input in the process of decision-making. (Stewart, 1990, p. 718)

This service was organized, Robin Murray and others have argued, by a clear link between Fordist methods of production and the social democratic state i.e. 'the idea of the standard product was given a democratic interpretation as the universal service to meet basic needs' (Murray, 1989). I want to review some of the features of a Fordist system of production to see if it fits this post-war modern service. Fordism is a way of describing a system of mass production designed to produce a standardized product, and it has these characteristics most associated with it: centralized planning, rigid organization, redesigned and directly managed tasks, flowline production and scale economics of production. A consequence of this system was the way in which the work of the employees was arranged; it was characterized by a mental–manual divide between workers and managers, fragmented and repetitive tasks, hierarchical organization and it was determined by rulebooks. It involved a high labour turnover, shopfloor resistance and growing unionization.

Teachers worked in a labour market defined by national salary scales, low unemployment and flattened promotion hierarchies; they were employed by steadily growing local and regional employers in an expanding system (in its early period) and trained uniformly. It could be argued that some of the Fordist methods of production were present in the post-war period i.e., bilateral schools, and their successors, the comprehensive schools, seem to have been popular choices in some country and urban areas because they allowed a wider provision of amenities with cheaper costs due to the scale of provision. In primary schools, it is not so easy to see the scale economics of production, perhaps this occurred in the relations of production in the immediate area. i.e., in the way the local authority developed, determined and rationalized its services around and in the primary schools. There was a rise in the hierarchies of work but this tended to appear as a simple set of hierarchies, replacing autocratic rule by headteachers. It is possible to see the schooling process as a system of flowline production especially as the school and the local organization of education services began to be seen as a whole (rather than as it was with the pre-war elementaries as an end in itself and delivered in a simple school system), however it was not a complex flowline system. Certainly this period is associated with widespread unionization in teaching and in its later decades, strong resistance by the unions and elements within them. Comprehensive schools had management structures (due to the scale and the task) which were complex; they had job redesigned functions, new specialization and skills, they were hierarchical and often bureaucratic.[3] The evidence on the production process is mixed. They were associated with experimentation (though this may not have been commonplace) and increased assessment; with quantity and with quality; with curriculum change and with prescription. It would be seen as an inadequate method of production — producing a standardized but flawed product, raising the quality of the standard product but not being able to create new and varied products if there was a demand for them. If the heightened form of Fordism within education is comprehensive schooling, the two forms (social democracy and its Fordist methods of mass production) declined together in education. The attack on comprehensivization was based on its standardization (lack of choice) and the ineffectiveness of its method of production (the quality of its product), both these criticisms were applied to other nationalized industries in this period, certainly the public service industries.

Yet in a post-war crisis of labour supply and of reconstruction, the teachers were able to develop an autonomy over aspects of their work. There was a constant post-war movement of unskilling teachers, with a very gradual rise in in-service courses, length of certification increases, post certificate and higher degrees and the creation of an all-degree entry into teaching. Exclusion of unskilled teachers was continually demanded. This seems at odds with a Fordist production system, dependent upon a split between the managers and workers; in this sense, Fordism was incomplete in schooling because there was an element of work, common in the public services, in which the employees were the implementers of the social democratic ideal themselves. They were partly creators of the system, not just the employees of it, for example, the influential National Association of Labour Teachers argued, in June 1952, that the establishment of comprehensive schools was a prerequisite for the creation of social democracy (Fenwick, 1976, p. 74). For example, the leading edge of comprehensive reform was composed of sections of teachers and one of its major arenas was in the main teacher union amongst the teachers or in the political and educational groups they were part of. The modernist professional debate over the form, content and purpose of education was one teachers took part in and also created. In other words the system of production was a byproduct of the social democratic reforms they began to support.

In education, the system began openly to fail when it could no longer deliver benefits to its partners or when its ideological foundations were impossible to sustain. The growth of alternative sources of expertise, Treasury controls and revenue crises, contraction and growing public sector unrest were all part of this decline of the corporate state in education. Collective bargaining was shaped by periods of economic restraint, by secret concordats on the acceptability of pay offers (from the Secretary of State for Education, the government minister in charge of the Department of Education) by a shift to public service block grants (and not special education grants), by the introduction of Department of Education and Science representatives in the process and, on the teachers' side, by the dominance of the majority union (and its priorities) in the negotiations. The official machinery, the national panel of employers and teachers (Burnham), began to lose its credibility as a forum for collective bargaining on pay as it became overshadowed by wider disputes over government pay policies and public expenditure cuts (Saran, 1989). The shape of collective bargaining post-war was increasingly dominated by central government pressures, intervention and regulation.

The intellectual origins of the key role for teachers in the creation of the modern, social democratic state lay in the writing of Webb (and others) but their practical origins lay in the war and post-war period; a period when mass production in Britain was at its height.

The Post-modern Teacher

The arrival of the market marks the end of the modern period. The functions of local education authorities are gradually displaced by agencies and input is replaced by output as the key evaluatory rule of education. In the ideology of the market, professionalism (or the degree of control exercised over work) may be viewed as neither beneficial nor co-optive; instead it is seen as an interference in the market or as an attempt at unfair monopoly by the teachers, part of the old corporatist state. So, professionalism is first seen, by the Right, as a form of producer capture of the public service. The modernist professional debate over the form, content and purpose of education was not translated to the post-Education Reform Act market. Professionalism as an employer discourse has almost entirely disappeared; this is a sign of its lack of positive significance to the new time. The overtones of a responsible group, working with the State, are no longer necessary or even valid. Teacher professionalism is now being redefined as a form of competent labour, flexible and multiskilled: it operates within a regulated curriculum and internal assessment system in a decentralized external school market. The dominant version is now a notion of individual responsibility and incentive reward legitimated by the Citizen's Charter idea of efficient service and performance incentive.[4] (Yet curriculum and professional autonomy were once linked closely together so that a reduction of control over the former was seen as inevitably weakening the latter.) The decentralization of the service has begun to redefine professionalism, for example in the Citizen's Charter it is already beginning to appear as defined by parent's rights and by the emphasis on efficient service. The Charter also links service standards and pay reward so that the idea of a professional standard of work is shifting; it is now seen as less of a collective responsibility of teachers than a matter of individual performance. The new Pay Review Body for teaching is part of the Charter strategy for all the public services. As the LEAs are moving away from direct control of schools and the school governors will be able to operate with some freedom in a local labour market, the Pay Review Body will guarantee the basic pay structure and differential strategy which has operated in the last few years.[5] It will be independent but only after being selected (mainly from industry), acting within the 'directions' given to it by the Secretary of State, to whom its recommendations must be acceptable. Without union negotiations local settlements could be made which will slow down or alter the market in teachers' labour (pay and conditions). It is also dependent upon a no-strike agreement.

The market in education raises the question of central control over teachers' pay in a more direct way than hitherto. The tensions in the Act between central regulation and supply and demand, seen in the National Curriculum and open enrolment, are not contradictory. Markets need strong regulation to operate effectively, for instance it needs regulatory laws which stop the labour force intervening in the market by acting in combination together. Teachers may only be in dispute with their own direct employers (under LMS[6], the governing body), may strike only with a secret ballot and may not engage lawfully in supporting colleagues elsewhere by engaging in a dispute at their school. Secondly, a restructuring of the workforce is going hand in hand with the change in the political economy of schools. Workforce flexibility is the shift government has encouraged; the trend is away from career development along salary scales (a consistent element of the older Burnham tradition) and into discretionary payments by management (allowances are now called selective payments), which over the last few years, have become a larger and larger element of the overall pay bill. The education market needs strong central control to make certain that the conditions exist for it to work. The move to a pay review body is a policy shift consistent with the need for central control.

In passing, it is worthwhile saying here that the open espousal of central control, including central funding of teacher pay, by the Conservatives is significant in itself. Indirect control of teachers or subtle external pressure is understandable but the political idea which underpinned collective bargaining between local employers and teacher association was that of a distinctively British democratic practice (see the post-war debates on British Government versus authoritarian governments) (Alexander, 1954). The untidiness of democratic negotiation is to be replaced by centrally imposed strategic management and its structures.

The driving force in this situation is not direct control intervention; as always, the British way of governance, at its most efficient, uses financial control, a simple regulatory framework and elite networks though the dominant metaphors or influences on this way of governing do alter, their purpose remains intact, even post-ERA. The leading edge of the required change looked likely to be the GMS and CTC[7] sectors which are allowed experimental conditions to change for example, they are not legally obliged to recognize teacher associations nor do they need to appoint or promote staff on the national conditions of service. However this view may need revising. The steering of the new system through the Review Body, the new Teacher Training Agency, the Schools Curriculum and Assessment Agency and by the Ofsted inspections, is probably sufficient to create a constantly shifting revolution of expectations, languages and practices which will drive the market system.

The Differentiated, Flexible Workforce in Teaching

Before this idea of the new differentiated teacher is developed, it is necessary to review the conditions which affect teachers' work under LMS. School governors will employ teachers, they will decide how many they need and decide job descriptions for them. They may decide the length of the teacher's contract (for a fixed period or permanent) and review annually the incentive allowances they award. School governors may try to persuade teachers to take on non-contractual duties, they may try to make teachers waive their statutory employment rights and they may discriminate against applicants for teaching posts and teachers in post. School governors will operate in a local educational market which may be unstable and so be unable to develop worthwhile forward planning. They may try to reassess their staffing structure and so try to economize by lowering salary levels, they can more easily reduce incentive payments. If their school is popular there will be more money available for allowances, enhancements and an extended local scale. If unpopular, teachers may well be made redundant. Teachers' pay involves several new differentiating features that school governors may use, creating staff flexibilities: teachers may start at a higher grade and go above the maximum scale, they may be fast tracked and given discretionary payments.

As the DES made clear some time ago, LMS meant far more than budgeting and accounting changes, it would enable

> governing bodies and headteachers to plan their use of resources — including their most valuable resource, their staff — to maximise effect in accordance with their own needs and priorities. As the DES made clear in several ways in the late 80s, the decentralization of the local education budget to schools was intended to focus on maximising resources, including the most valuable resource, the teachers.

School governors are the direct, local employers of the school teachers in their school, even though the LEA has residual responsibility for them. They will act like school owners and the teachers will be their workforce. In other words, they are near the time when they can pay teachers what they want (within this broad setting) and certainly reward teachers differently for the same work. Even without a great movement into pay flexibility and a resistance to the idea of class there is a concern being raised about two aspects of it, firstly, the idea of a 'loser' class in teaching and secondly, a redefinition of work which will allow an increase in 'unskilled' teaching. The loser class points the way to groups of teachers who will lose out in the market. There is an expectation that current inequalities in teaching will continue as LMS is about differentiation of the workforce, and so it is likely that groups of women teachers and black teachers will continue to lose out in pay, promotion or recruitment. (This is a serious concern about LMS and should be as important a focus for research as the idea of reward.) The loser class aren't necessarily ineffective or less hard working than other teachers but will receive neither promotion nor professional training. This loser class may be 25–30 per cent of the profession, according to one research project. They lose out in the secondary schools because men in shortage subjects get allowances and in the primary because there are fewer allowances. They were retreating into the classroom with

> a pervasive sense of bewilderment and frustration at a system which did not, as they saw it, recognise their virtues, reward their efforts or offer any help with their future career. (*TES*, 12.10.91)

The gap between these teachers and new multiskilled teachers (the supervisory or middle management created by highly managed schools) could grow.

The second aspect of LMS is the new emphasis on workforce flexibility. New routes into teaching, which may be school-based training, or shortened training courses or transfer of untrained staff from different sectors (further education in particular) will add to the differentiation of the workforce and (if historical precedent is anything to go by) create tensions between them. The idea of a skilled teacher (seen as a graduate or certificated teacher in times when many others weren't) has been crucial to the debates about professionalism and unionism and the tendency has been in recent decades to fight for the upskilling of the employed semi-skilled teacher and to fight against the employment of new routes for the unskilled or semi-skilled teacher. This was easier during the post-war project of an improving education service, not so easy in a service fragmented and marked by inequality.

The Audit Commission, a government body with a duty to ensure efficient services in health and local government reported on LMS (1991) and emphasized this idea of a differentiated workforce in a new way. Expressing it quite bluntly at one point, it argues that with a fixed budget school governors might decide to employ (unskilled/semi-skilled) classroom assistants not teachers 'at least two classroom assistants might be employed full-time for the cost of one teacher' (p. 32). Indeed the whole emphasis of the report appears to be on the 'flexible delivery' of primary education by the use of untrained labour. They suggest that school governors (through their teachers) 'delegate' tasks to untrained assistants in the schools, such as clerical work, low-grade supervision and pupil groupwork.

Professional expertise, in line with HMI thinking, is increasingly defined as a supervisory skill and it will be used to supervise semi-skilled or unskilled workers in the classroom.[8] These people will be 'locally available' and suitable to be recruited as teachers ('licensed and articled teacher' p. 33) and as classroom assistants and their employment (the cost of it compared to 'real' teachers) will depend upon the amount of (free) parental cooperation within the school (p. 33). The report carries on in this mode with reference to part-time teachers, job share opportunities and supply teachers (a 'flexible resource' p. 28). The labour market for teachers will be affected by local conditions of employment and their own employment, scale and discretionary payouts will be judged, in part, against the cost of employing local untrained or partly-trained labour. Recent publications by the Inspectorate and by a DfE commissioned project have both emphasized the new roles in school for non-teacher staff (HMI, 1992; Mortimore, *et al.*, 1993).

The Redesigned Teacher?

In this section, I want to examine a possible congruency between the new labour process in teaching and its Post-Fordist or Taylorist features. If the post-war period was characterized by mass production and a consequent 'common sense' in education fixed on scale economics, standardization, work hierarchies etc., all of which in practice affected teaching as work, then in what way will the new ways of producing shape teaching? According to Murray (1989), post-Fordist production is characterized by economics of scope (wide product range) rather than scale, flexibility of production and of labour rather than fixed scales and duties, centralized control over decentralized work rather than bureaucratic hierarchies, contracted-out functions rather than in-house services, core/periphery workforce rather than single status work and the rise of part-time workers rather than full-time workers.

This description (or catalogue of features) could be used to develop a series of hypotheses or sensitizing concepts in researching schools. They are not to be read off from industrial practices or correspondence directly sought but prevailing industrial models percolate, cross pollinate or are just plainly applied by policy makers searching for practical ways to make policies work. Of course decisions about policies are contained within the same determining discourse as the solution. It was unlikely in a period of state nationalization and corporate organizations that education would move into decentralized autonomous sectors. Some homology of solution is to be expected. New technologies which allow the fast collection and analysis of data in the distribution sector are unlikely to bypass the education sector as new markets for tested products increase profitability.

Post-Fordism might be a description of a practice or even a rationalizing discourse for multiple random effects; it might only refer to some particular kinds of new industries. Yet it is beginning to look as if it could act as a description of work practices in primary or secondary education. For example, there appears to be the growing capacity for a wider product range to be developed (within the new range of schools in the secondary sector), there are strong controls built into the system (viz. the structure of the National Curriculum and its assessment) and financial controls operating which can guide the system (viz. the Pay Review Body) funding formulas for schools, in-service (teacher courses) funding targets etc., and there is an emphasis on contracted-out functions (certainly in building and maintenance). Secondary schools seem to be investing a greater proportion of their budget in marketing themselves externally but it doesn't look as if many primary schools are yet engaged in market research. One of the most interesting features of the shift is in teachers' work. While commentators, especially in education management, tend to announce the arrival of teamwork fairly regularly now, and may even refer to statutory control which makes its arrival imminent (Busher and Saran, 1992), there is reference to it in job descriptions and in management models in school development plans. The new good teacher is without doubt to be described as a teamworker but evidence of a qualitative shift in work relations rather than a quantitative shift in worktime is still thin. Some of the tendencies described by Murray appear to be at work in schools. The schools have become the point at which personnel changes, the employment of contractors, the speed of production are being managed, a post-1988 phenomenon. The jury is still out on the flexibility of production, a key post-Fordist measure, but there appears to be a new flexibility of planning, of classroom use, of workgroups and of pupil organization.

Stuart Hall argued that the transition between methods of production (from mass to batch production) would be characterized by unevenness, contradictory outcomes, disjunctures, delays, overlapping emergent projects and so forth (Hall, 1989). This is certainly the case in schooling; it is not easy to distinguish these changes, never mind work out their trajectory. However he asks 'where is the leading edge of the change?' The gradual diminution of LEA services and their contracting-out, the creation of school budgets and local markets, the centralization of curriculum and assessment, the specification of in-service training priorities, the rise of a probable core/periphery workforce in schools (permanent teachers versus part-time and classroom assistants), the impending differentiation of schools and pupils — all these suggest that the leading edge may be shifting from parts of the post-school sector into secondary/primary schooling. Schools appear to have elements of the old and new. The reliance on classrooms as the main unit of production can obscure the rapidity of other changes in their work. Indeed Robin Murray has argued that these changes in the public sector are not post-Fordist but an extension of Taylorism, a Fordist method of increasing production efficiencies, into the work of the previously untouched professional workers.

> Jobs have been broken down and the less skilled parts assigned to lower paid workers (this has been at the heart of nursing) . . . Systems of reward have been measured, and individual cash payments promoted as the main form of incentive . . . There has been likewise a restructuring of managerial control. Service are (now) run at arm's length on the basis of a performance agreement. Ministerial and senior bureaucratic responsibility is now confined to issuing contracts and the monitoring of performance. (Murray, 1989)

Even though there may be positive features in the new forms of work, control of teachers' work will continue to be a dominant aspect of these forms. So, Murray may be right about teaching, within the public services, and work hypotheses will have to be addressed not only to the range and resemblances in the shifts in work but their capacity to control teachers efficiently and effectively.

Redesigning Work, Creating a New Professionalism

In this paper, I have discussed the restructuring of teachers' work and a relationship between work and professionalism in the modern system of education and in the emerging market, suggesting that the leading edge of the new labour process is unevenly post-Fordist but that a new differentiated, flexible teaching force is emerging.

Redesign: Teachers are developing new skills in pedagogy and assessment, new subject expertise, specialist functions of supervision over staff, new job descriptions and a developmental planning process in the school. The consequence of these changes is that, in a practical sense, the work has been redesigned. This change can be seen within primary schools where the idea of the good primary teacher has shifted from being an isolated classroom worker with generalist skills to a classroom and school-based team worker with specialist skills (Lawn, 1988a). The job is capable of a separation into parts which differentially trained or employed people will teach and that it is redefined as a whole school (not just class) competency.

The national context of this redesign is that the national pay bargaining structures have been dissolved and a new Pay Review Body for teachers' pay has encouraged the development of a pay flexibility, built around permanent and temporary allowances, which have shifted the emphasis from basic or standard pay for all teachers to incentive payments for a proportion of teachers which will probably be extended into a merit pay system (Lawn and Whitty, 1992). Finding ways of connecting performance, productivity and reward will be the leading edge of future changes.

Local Management of Schools will mean that a local labour market is created through low income generation and a consequent loss of teachers, and vice versa. In effect, a teachers' hiring fair has already begun, with individuals bargaining (if that is not too strong a word) for their pay.

New Professionalism: Two parallel developments are taking place in teaching which appear to support contradictory explanations about teachers' work. Firstly, there is a sense of empowerment or increased job satisfaction which is currently emerging out of empirical research and appears to be associated with a new range of skills and responsibilities (Campbell, 1991). This is contradictory itself as extensive evidence produced in this report for the intensification and extensive nature of teachers' work is overridden with an interpretation determined to downplay evidence of deskilling, viz.

> . . . the imposed change of the national curriculum, far from deskilling and deprofessionalising teachers, was on the contrary seen by them as extending their skills and increasing their professionalism . . . (particularly) leading to improved planning of teaching and extending collaboration with their colleagues, especially in the development of whole school approaches to the curriculum and its assessment. (p. 7)

Secondly, there is evidence of a fragmentation of teaching, not only through the continuance of a major group of teachers (a supposed loser class) but of new kinds of teachers and classroom assistants. These new teacher are acting, within the labour market, as flexible workers as opposed to the new core workers, the multiskilled teachers. Both these groups, the new teachers and the multiskilled teachers, should be taken together in the analysis, there is a deskilling and an upskilling process happening.

It is worth recollecting that the version of the teacher that is being re-designed is individualistic not collective in orientation, differentiated not homogeneous, competent not responsible. From the employer's point of view, professionalism would be seen as an individual attribute, something the teacher has or will acquire.

To review my arguments and excursions, the old idea of progress has gone: it was built on an alliance between social democracy, modernism and Fordism, and teachers were woven through this alliance and ultimately de-moralized by the consequent labour process and the arguments around it, underfunding and the lack of power of their representatives. They lost confidence as the faults of the Fordist model became evident in its industrial base and as a social democratic momentum, built on growth, faltered. They lost the dream of the collegial comprehensive and the progressive, comprehensive primary for the reality of a bureaucratic, mass school. Although post-Fordism offers some hope to some teachers of a collegial teamwork or a multiskilled work, this will take place in the context of yearly budgeting (pitting teacher costs against each other) and a new semi-skilled and differentiated workforce. New ideas of school management (offering 'a new collegiality, shared whole school planning and flexible work') could have the same effect on teachers as it is doing in single status, total quality management environments where the employees trade the union for some level of participation in decision-making and financial incentives.

It is not clear whether new, local work environments in teaching will create an opportunity for teachers. Post-Fordist analysts are clearer on the demise of Fordism, its regime of accumulation and its mode of regulation (Allen, 1993) than on the opportunities within post-Fordism. The end of progress for professionals can be seen more clearly elsewhere, for example, in the TQM style work of Silicon Valley, where it now means a total orientation towards work and career and an abrogation of personal and collective responsibility of the social purpose and meaning of work (Hayes, 1990). Teacher professionalism is based on ideological and material conditions and so while the post-war, modern version of professionalism emerged with its associated labour process and is now in decline, versions of the post-modern professionalism in teaching are only lightly discernible. The conditions for a new kind of work, stripped of 'progress', fragmented, contained within a local environment and centrally determined are in place.

Notes

1 Teacher professionalism is not a fixed idea, it is situational and relational, it has contradictory aspects (progressive and conservative) and it is not homogeneous.
2 Fordist production is characterized as a system of mass production, sustained by mass markets; in this paper the term Fordism is used to describe the pervasive influence of ideas of mass production and its associated labour process in 'industries' outside the mass manufacturing sector. (see Sayer, A., 1989, 'Post-Fordism in question' *International Journal of Urban and Regional research*, vol. 13, no. 4.)
3 This contrasts with the image of the comprehensive sold to teachers as a collegial institution, a form of professional advancement, contrasted with unionization (CCCS, 1981, *Unpopular Education*, Hutchinson.)
4 The Citizen's Charter operates across the public services and is a 1990s Conservative policy which views the citizen as a consumer and defines performance indicators for the user of all public services, sometimes rather crudely.
5 The Pay Review Body is the post collective bargaining (Burnham) panel which decides the broad framework under which teachers are paid. It is strongly influenced by government direction and under direct appointment. It currently focuses upon merit and flexible pay for teachers.
6 Local Management of Schools means the delegation of budgets from the LEA to the school and the decentralization of decision-making in key areas, notably on staffing and pay.
7 Grant-maintained School means a school where parents have voted to leave or opt-out from the local authority schools and in to direct financing from the DES. A City Technology College is a secondary school with a specialist curriculum, usually vocational, which were supposed to be financed privately, by industry, but were mainly paid for by the Government. There are few of them.

8 Her Majesty's Inspectors, the central inspectorate of schools, have also been reorganized (and reduced) into Ofsted (a regulatory body, similar to those for the water, gas and electricity industries).

10 Second Guessing the Past: Organizing in the Market

Old certainties about the traditions and prospects of teacher unions have eroded in the last decades leaving traces on a fast altering landscape. The confident histories of their past, full of dramatic struggle or quietly successful negotiations, detailing the victory of the teachers over recalcitrant employers and the steady success of this or that campaign, appear now to be a stage in their development, a finished period in their history. The unions were closely attached in Europe to the rise of the modernist and social democratic state and owed more to the parallel rise of the labour movements than many of their members recognized. Questions about their future in the world of the market will also raise questions about their past.

Through a study of the past of teacher unionism in England and a frugal use of a recent American theory about the stages of teacher unionism, the relation of a union to control and to work will be explored. Propositions about the key factors in teacher unionism — context, identity, contradiction, competition and work organization — which shape teachers' professional associations will be produced instead other than the idea of stages. An exploration of possible courses of action open to teacher unions, within the context of regulation and market, will be based on the past and on inferences about the present.

Explaining the Past: Unions, Work and Stages of Development

The range and depth of the current restructuring of the education industry raises questions about the response of the unions, indeed it raises questions about the continuing effective existence of teacher unions. The development of teacher unionism and collective bargaining has not been an area of close study for researchers in general. Most of the analysis, preceding the 1980s, assumed, in describing England and Wales, that a steady state of development had occurred in which the unions would co-exist in partnership with the central and local government. This view is most clearly expressed by Asher Tropp, (Tropp, 1957) writing in the 1950s, from within a large project, based at the London School of Economics, on occupational groups and the middle classes. The development of organized teachers or the 'profession' was bound up with State policies, he argued

It [the profession] was created by the State and in the 19th Century the State was powerful enough to claim almost complete control over the teachers and to manipulate his status while at the same time disclaiming all responsibility towards him. Slowly and as the result of prolonged effort, the organised profession has won free and has reached a position of self-government and independence. (Tropp, 1957, p. 3)

From within the context of the 1950s this commonsense view of teacher unionism made sense. Gone were the sporadic strikes of the 1920s and left-wing extremists had been expelled from many schools, education was being rebuilt and extended with cross-party support and the moderation and experience of many local teachers were being used by their local employers in these changes. In common with other histories of education which preceded his own, Tropp was describing a liberal history of development, built on a metaphor of 'spreading light', which was really no more than a commonsense view of education from within a quiet period of social consensus and economic stability. Tropp's explanation leaves a lot to be desired; for example, exactly how did the State come to allow a key occupational group a position of independence or exactly how does an occupational group, over a long period of time, develop a consistency of approach in achieving an agreed set of goals? Taking this latter point further, Tropp was in effect arguing that various strikes, pay campaigns, economic and political alliances and a cross-party non-political interest group approach over a timespan of a hundred years was all part of a conscious effort to achieve occupational freedom. This remarkable campaign was achieved either with the State's blessing or by force of arms and argument. This is a difficult argument to develop, it is ahistorical and positivist, held together only by the social and political circumstances of its time (Lawn and Ozga, 1981). However, for the moment, this explanation of professional association and occupational groups as key agents of educational power will be taken at face value and will be used here to make a number of points. Firstly, although there may be an assumption that unionism has moved through several stages in its representation of teachers as an occupational group, it is not clear what they were. Secondly, teacher unionism is involved with the policy-making of the State and the success of the union is bound up with the intentions of the State toward it. Thirdly, that the ideas and education policies of a particular period shape the view of teacher unionism promoted by commentators. (This last point is worth bearing in mind as arguments for a new unionism are produced.)

So, in effect, there is a clear sense in which the union, as part of an occupational strategy, gained considerable power but little sense about how this worked. The generality of the argument leaves the condition of teachers' work, the debates and organizing in the union and the negotiations with employers and policy makers obscured. Although Tropp does not argue a stage theory, it is clear that the achievement of collective bargaining (the Burnham panel) in the 1920s signified the start of the union's power, the aloofness from direct political alliances another important step.

Recent scholarship in the United States takes one aspect of Tropp's enquiry further and tries to develop a model of unionization stages (Kerchner and Mitchell, 1988). Three stages are suggested. The first stage is called 'Meet and Confer'; this is a pre-bargaining stage in which organized teachers had the right to present demands to their employers and discuss them even if, in practice, custom, law and their own propriety made acting upon these demands difficult. The second stage (or generation) is called 'Good Faith Bargaining' and is characterized by teacher solidarity and employee welfare demands developed in a collective or industrial bargaining process, using collective contracts and conflict management procedures. The third stage is embryonic, it is seen as a period of negotiation and problem-solving by unions and employers and the rediscovery of an accountable professionalism. Before discussing the problems of a possible new stage of unionism, the very idea of a stage or generation unionism needs further analysis.

A stage theory implies some level of theoretical explanation across sites, periods and societies. It was not the obligation of Kerchner and Mitchell to write such a cross-cultural history of teacher unionism but it would be ill-advised to move from the distinctive North American theorizing and context of their stages of unionism and to extrapolate it into other societies and their own significant histories. It is a theory based in North America in two ways, it uses a history of development based on specific cities and school districts and it uses particular theories of explanation grounded in American political theorizing. At a distance it is difficult to determine the specificity of American examples cited as cases of a developmental unionism or the historical periods to which the general stages are attached; the latter appears to be firstly, pre-1960s, secondly, 1960–80s and thirdly, late 1980s onward. Some similarities may be drawn between the advances of the National Union of Teachers and its relations with government in the first half of the century in which terms like 'Meet and Confer' or 'Good Faith Bargaining' might have some purchase. The events might appear to be similar, for example, a local association petitioning its council employers for a pay rise in the early part of the century, but they could only be described as similar if the conceptual framework used by the writers are shared. Michael Barber produced an English stage model of teacher unionism, drawn from a reading of a number of histories, in which he argued that there were three main stages, Conflict, Partnership and a return to Conflict; his version of the future, strategic unionism, I will return to later. Collective bargaining was certainly significant in this model as it underpinned the great period of partnership and broke down in the final period of Conflict. Barber uses governmental relations, like Tropp, to signal that it was not only a question of employer–employee relations which counted in the construction of stages but the relation of teachers to the State, particularly a concern for control and power, which shaped political policies and aims. My own view, tentatively expressed in stages, is mainly influenced by the idea of conflict over the control of work, its purpose and structure, between employers and government and the teachers, through their unions. Collective bargaining or

Table 10.1: Three models of teacher unionism

	KERCHNER and MITCHELL	BARBER	LAWN
Stage One	MEET and CONFER pre-1960s	CONFLICT 1910–1925	MARKET pre-1920s
Stage Two	GOOD FAITH BARGAINING 1960s-1980s	PARTNERSHIP i. 1925–44 ii. 1944–70	COLONIAL /CORPORATE 1920s-mid 1980s
Stage Three	NEGOTIATED POLICY late 1980s-	CONFLICT 1970–90	REGULATION and MARKET

the market would only be seen as temporary solutions to problems of control and economy. There is no golden age or sense of progressive development in education management which appears to be present in the other two columns. Certainly, there is no sense of a clear next stage nor the progressive possibilities it may contain.

The point of perspective for each model is very different. In which case, what value does a stage theory have as a predictor of future union responses or policies? A crucial part of Kerchner and Mitchell's theory of union development is the idea of inter-generational conflict, (the internal dynamic of the union); this appears to reduce human endeavour and disagreement to a decontextualized ritual display, a form of in-group and out-group conflict behaviour related to power in the organization. Geared around 'basic interests', it is a movement between a status quo, the generation in power, and its opposition. Although this battle is seen as political and may involve a new ideology or belief system justifying the actions of the players, the organization is politicized only in the sense that all actions, meetings, conversations, etc. are seen as political. This limits the idea of politics to single questions of inter-personal power and individual and group self-interests. This micropolitical analysis is busy but inadequate. Are political actions and ideas reducible to power relations in organizations (Morgan, 1986)? My analysis of periods of teacher union history in the UK suggests that politics and ideology are not just the symbols of conflict, they have associations beyond the union and involve positioned teacher identities (Lawn, 1987a and b). They are often related to general conditions of employment and political and social ideas common to a period and indeed, they are used to explain the changes in the State or management or the restructuring of capital. To divorce these ideas from their time, the actual material conditions and the policy changes is to lose the dynamic context of unionism and replace it with *ersatz* rituals.

Conflict happens within the union about conditions prevailing in teachers' work and the best way to alleviate or change them. Union history has many such instances, evident at annual national conferences; in England and Wales it is much more likely that the national conferences were seen as the place for debate on new policies and that the debaters were part of large groups of teachers organized into political alliances. Those political alliances have been Centre-Left (and now perhaps versions of the Left) since the 1950s. (This is similar to the French model where unions are organized over significant kinds of left politics) (Duclaud-Williams). A model of teacher unionism that assumes politics means micro-political analysis is missing a key dimension. The shadowy concept of the State plays a significant role in Tropp and none in Kerchner and Mitchell. In the history of teacher unionism in England the State has been a significant factor affecting the conditions of work, the role of collective bargaining, the stages of development and, importantly, the ideologies (educational/political) subscribed to in the union organizational conflicts. Government has, at different times, encouraged local pay settlements, discouraged them and favoured a joint wage council, circumscribed the work of the council by limiting money for settlements and disbanded the council and pay negotiation. As the main provider of teacher salaries, albeit indirectly, it controlled the processes the unions had to try to influence. Also its controlling methods have been very sophisticated, including the colonial government method of indirect rule (using 'independent' local employers as agents or barriers) and by means of its own version of ideology, the idea of professionalism and service. A model of teacher unionism that excludes the State in England would be left with very little explanatory power.

Key Ideas for the Study of Teacher Unionism

What factors or sensitizing concepts may be used to analyse teacher unionism at any one period or event, to determine either a developmental view of their history or a better case understanding of their actions? The first is that teaching and other forms of work are often homologous. It is possible but rather fruitless to study teaching as a separate sort of craft or work with little in common with any other, and to view the employment of teachers as different to other kinds of business, industry or service sector. Teaching appears to have a lot in common with other kinds of work. The treatment of its majority, women teachers, in terms of low salary scales, poor promotion and a marriage bar was similar, in the pre-war period, to that of women civil servants. Trends in the teaching labour process, described as intensification of work, de-skilling and proletarianization, are similar to those in many other kinds of work, as are the methods, seen in the social construction of skill, used to deal with them. Teaching has its own equivalents to rate-busting and to go-slows! The correspondence that is claimed here is partly the result of a consistency of government policy, national or local, as to the cheapness or efficiency of the system, partly the result of a governmental ideology, spread through the departments of state (viz. 'partnership' or 'market' or 'industrial bargaining' or 'social contract') and partly the borrowing in education from alternative ways of organizing (from educational ideas to industrial practice) (Apple, 1990, Ozga and Lawn, 1988).

The second point is about control. Teachers are not just employees, they are state employees with obligations to national priorities. They are often the subject of moral panics derived from industrial rivalry abroad or social unrest at home; it is teachers and their training that are often the focus for tighter controls or a new restructuring. They can be seen as a social danger, a whole group of potentially destabilizing agents in the social fabric. This happens when there is a fear by a ruling group that its hold is slipping or when teachers join radical (left) groups. Control is important and though it may be in tension with economic policy it has to be recreated. In at least two major ways this century, control has been developed in a very complex way regarding teachers. First, financial controls were tightened after curriculum controls were dismantled and a new ideology of service (professionalism) was produced. Secondly, while financial controls were tight, immediate responsibility was offered to teachers locally in reconstructing education and an ideology of partnership was constructed explaining this licensed consensus. The political and social context of control, or its 'negotiated' order in a period or situation, are important in understanding the particular necessity of the overall strategy. The more centralized and overt the control over teachers, the more likely that they will engage in political campaigns with opposition groups to counter state influence. In and out of these two factors weaves professionalism. Appeals to responsibility or declarations of independence may be directly suffixed by acute economic crises in which teachers are laid off. A strategy may have contradictions and professionalism is an example of that. In recent teachers' action, productivity was the key word and professionalism (even in reproof) obscure, yet now in a period of managing severe change professionalism and its attendants (a possible Teaching Council, etc.) are vocal and the Gradgrinds are becoming quieter. This is the official professionalism, it exists in the same form but with a different function and meaning when teachers use it.

The third factor is the membership; who are the teachers? In the main teacher union in England, the NUT, different constituent groups appear to have had a substantial effect on policy at any one time. For example, male teachers, urban and rural, excluded women teachers from the full rights of union membership or class teachers, as an organized group, gradually declined in direct influence at the time left-wing groups of teachers rose. Smaller teacher unions have grown based on sectional interests, these interests have affected the way they approach collective bargaining. For example, a male teachers' union, the NAS, was created which was militant in its defence of 'men teachers for boys' and with this claim tried to determine its share of the labour market, and so the remuneration and welfare of its members. Their entry into collective bargaining, and their exclusion from it by dominant unions, created a constant process of attrition and militancy, only partly directed at employers. Is it possible for different teacher unions to have different core ideas and that these may be congruent or not with dominant employment ideology. A further point on membership is that the ideas that drive teachers to organize are not utilitarian, they are often embedded in their very identity as teachers; that is, they teach this way, they have these values, they have had a career like this and this is their association — with like-minded people. Ideas are not just a useful expression of discontent with leadership or a 'secular gospel' on defending basic interests, they are a core expression of being a teacher and being in association with others. The strength of these ideas even affects the way they combine and cannot be separated from wider sets of ideas circulating and resonating in the wider society. For example, a feminist teachers' union began as an expression of discontent with the main teachers union and its practices and as a combination of ex-suffragettes and other first wave feminists. Its approach to organization was based on a close sisterhood and supportive networks which never varied and seemed to exclude faction-fighting and generational conflict (King, 1987). Is an idea of generational conflict, built on a rather weak notion of nuclear family life, the only imagery possible of union development and does it exclude other ways of acting? Teachers' union membership in England may often be an expression of their social, political and educational ideas and as teaching is often an expression of improvement (pedagogically to politically), social reconstructionist ideas of the Left and other sources have flowed into the union through its membership (as once did the ideas of the Church teachers). Teachers have organized in the union and organized the union in pursuit of these ideas.

The union is a contested idea. In 'The Idea of Teacher Unionism' union politics appear to be responses to employer acts, expressed as generational conflicts in the union which occur at the margin of the stages and as an inter-generational organization micro-politics. But if these limited expressions of union politics are placed to one side in understanding English teacher union development (as the theoretical manifestation of particular North American cultural ideas), then we are still left with a concept of some theoretical value. The union is seen as the expression of an idea/ideas in process of transformation, it is a contested concept, it is not fixed. In this sense their work stands as a critique of Tropp whose own analysis saw teachers as using a constant occupational strategy, without deviation, over time. It is also an historically accurate notion of unionism and the deep debates over courses of action, allies and politics. The problem for the researcher is to look for signs of the competing versions of values and beliefs (even 'secular gospels') expressed within debate and action as part of responses to employer policies and to see if, in particular periods or localities or disputes, new ideas appear to be winning out. However, this rather Hegelian analysis must be tempered by reference to processes of economic determination and state control which will need other forms of analysis.

Teachers were the first major group of white collar workers to organize into professional association in England. They are organized yet association membership is not, and never really has been, stable. Within one union, or between them, there is a market for teacher membership. It is partly based on insurance policies, school traditions or school sector, qualifications or job hierarchies and, of course, on policies and traditional identity. Union membership is influenced by gender, and this has been a major organizing factor in the past, creating new unions and shaping the responses of other unions. This idea of a shifting union membership, defined by the educational politics of a period and by the changes in the workforce and working condition, is an important one. Unions are not major stable blocs in a system description but they are always changing; they are vehicles for consistent policies and sites of contradictory ones; they define themselves against another union and against their employers. Like any social organization they are also shaped by the dominant ideas and policies in time, especially as they reshape the work of teaching, change teachers' pay and conditions and the places in which they work.

As an example of the relationship between union membership and the organization of the teachers' work, the early history of the NUT is of interest. In its first years, the NUT only organized certificated teachers and it excluded other kinds of teachers, the uncertificated, supplementary, pupil teacher and probationary teachers. Also it only organized within elementary schools and not from within the large private and secondary schools. Although from the outset the NUT discussed its claims in terms of a 'professional dignity', it was organized as a craft union. On the one hand it used its formidable legal department to try to intimidate small local education authorities and school managers, and on the other it tried to restrict the supply of teachers. Craft unions organized to maintain or raise their standard of living by trying to control the supply of workers rather than allow the employers to control the supply. In this way they felt they could protect the value of their craft skill. By professionalism, the union appeared to mean the employment of certificated teachers and the exclusion of semi-skilled or unskilled teachers. Although the union had recruited many of the certificated teachers, there were about 80 000 other teachers in elementary schools, all employed at cheaper rates and their number was growing in a time of shortage. At this time the craft policy of exclusion and professionalism left many teachers unorganized and hostile to the NUT. The main elements of its policy were to control entry into teaching by means of a register, to reduce the amount of employer interference into teachers' duties and work, to gain job security, adequate salaries (including a scale of salaries) and a pension.

The arguments within a union, not just between the unions, is of importance. Towards the end of this period, the NUT moved from its craft identity to an identity closer to an industrial union. It began to recruit uncertificated teachers, faced with a rapid growth in their number and a recognition that strikes could not be run by a small elite alone. Yet this internal shift in the NUT caused the creation of the NAS; in its early days this union was determined to keep alive the old craft policy although, this time, it defined it more openly as a policy of male ascendancy. They then competed for male teachers from that point on. Although this period was highly significant in the development of union policies its use here is meant to illustrate the factors which work to create those policies and which change the nature of the association. So, teachers' professional associations are shaped by a number of factors — homologies with other kinds of work, controls and oppositions, membership stability, social and political context, teacher identity, contradiction, interunion competition and work organization. Although these analytical categories might complicate the task of creating stages of development, they are necessary in understanding the way in which teacher unions grew and declined in England.

The Union in the Present

A New Kind of Work?

If there is a relation between changes in work and the teacher unionism, then it is necessary to return to a description of work in the 1990s. Although it is an error to look at policy as if it is the same as operational reality, nonetheless in England and Wales the development of government policies in the late 1980s produced an education system in change and turmoil. There have been a number of incongruencies in government education policy (Jones, 1989) due to the different conservative pressure groups and alliances but by the late 1980s the idea of the market dominated educational policy. The market is intended to operate in a number of ways; it will allow popular schools to open their enrolment, it will create new categories of schools (with some private funding), it will allow some diversity between schools (by means of devolved management) and it will allow teacher salaries to depend on supply and demand (in specialisms or low-cost regions). The idea of a market in education is not an idea peculiar to the governing of education, it is an ideological key stone of government policy in private and public sectors of industry (Ball, 1990). It is closely associated with the privatizing of nationalized industries and with the decentralized management structures of the new, market-led multinationals which have grown in the 1980s. However what the market means as the dominant explanatory discourse of education and what it means in the regulatory practices of government appear to be different. The high visibility of market speak is paralleled by the low visibility of market regulation, ditto high visibility of market metaphors and the low visibility of market exclusions. There has been a quiet exclusion of teacher unions from the languages of the market, so that unions appear to be sidelined and then represented as the past.

A market needs strong social regulation and centralization to guarantee the conditions for its success even though it is spoken of as freeing the system from regulation and controls. Consequently, throughout the last few years (the early 1990s) the new discursive practice of the market has needed to work with regulation to manage the creation of market practices. Teachers' work has had to be restructured. Teachers' conditions of work have been made more 'flexible'; new detailed job descriptions specify new broader skills and responsibilities, new directed duties and time control. Also, the curriculum and its assessment are clearly and exhaustively specified and teachers will be monitored and appraised more closely. Each school has a delegated budget, including a salaries budget, so that school governors and the headteacher will now be more closely connecting salary, duties and employment and making decisions about productivity (Lawn, 1988a). The effectiveness, the popularity and the costs of schools will be monitored closely at the national level by inspectors and officials.

This conceptualization and management of education borrows its ideas from two related sources, the right-wing market economics of Hayek (Johnson, 1989) as mediated by policy groups close to government and the new management ideas current in British and multinational (including franchise) businesses where the emphasis is on strong centralized controls (in accounting, profit calculation, just in time production etc.) and decentralized units of production and management. Ideas of the new management, such as the flexible workforce, human resource management, individual contracts and tight budgeting are now moving into education (Lawn, 1988a). For teachers this will mean a new definition of their work, skills and duties within a work culture altered to team-based and intra-supervised teaching and a regional and national setting composed of inspection, efficiency checks and competition. A new 'good' teacher will be in the making. This is not just a new movement in work with its own language, but a radical shift away from the post-war system, described as partnership and professionalism within a democratic consensus. Although very frayed, this idea was forged in the wartime and post-war reconstruction of education; a clear vision of a democratic society with a relatively straightforward view of the teachers and their associations (Lawn and Ozga, 1986). A new reality is being created in which the role of the unions is not very clear.

A New Kind of Unionism?: Control and Work

If stage is the right word, then at what stage are the relations between teachers, through their associations, and their managers/employers in the quasi-market of education in the 1990s? What suggestion is there that a new stage of unionism has been reached? In Kerchner and Mitchell's book it appears that a new generation of unionists, along with employers in some key cities, are arguing within the union for a change to a third or professional unionism stage. These authors suggest that if they aren't arguing for change then they ought to be. Professional unionism moves out from collective bargaining to areas of professional self-government and school productivity as a solution to the negative effects of industrial unionism *and* the school as an effective educational organization. Government policies in England, created with similar problems in mind, look somewhat different. Avoiding collective bargaining was a step taken through the market not a new revamping of unionism. The market solution was taken before the creation of a new, revised version of professionalism. So, while the problem might be similar the solutions look very different.

The idea of reform unionism comes out of the demands of city politics in the USA and is fuelled by the need to create new solutions to the fiscal crises of urban areas and to the problems of raising local taxes for education when it is perceived to be failing. The demands of the local economy for new kinds of worker and the national agenda for retaining dominant global economic status fuel the reform of education. Decentralization of power to schools is matched by new definitions of their responsibilities. However, what is missing in the logic of change arguments, linked to professional unionism in the USA, is a sense of the regularities in the governing/managing of teachers which are present in the English landscape. There are two aspects which are central to this point: the first is through the necessity to control, regardless of the particular system features, and the second is the forms of work available elsewhere and used as a language and a practice, changing teachers' work in school.

Control is a central issue in the politics of education in England. The issue is not control over teachers and schools but how, at any one time, controls are devised, shaped or operated. The relation between control and collective bargaining, through the special Burnham panel, created in the early 1920s, is complex. A system which can be described as a partnership between teachers, local and central government could so effectively because of the existence of Burnham. Burnham was the symbolic sign of the partnership at work. It wasn't always easy but it was in existence. Apart from the Schools Council (in the late 1960s and 1970s), there was no other significant forum where teacher associations met with local government leaders, with central government officers in close attendance. Control was not absolute but it operated, with increasing difficulty, through this panel and its networks. The end of collective bargaining in the late 1980s meant the end of a certain kind of union organization, an unstable future for national teacher pay and conditions and the possible demise of unions as key players in the education service.

The post-war restructuring of education strengthened the role of collective bargaining. At the same time although LEAs remained technically the employer of most teachers, an ever-increasing proportion of funding for education, particularly teacher salaries, came from central government. Collective bargaining was shaped by periods of economic restraint, by secret concordats on the acceptability of pay offers (from the Secretary of State) by a shift to public service block grants (and not special education grants), by the introduction of DES representatives in the process and, on the teachers' side, by the dominance of the majority union (and its priorities) in the negotiations. Burnham began to lose its credibility as a forum for collective bargaining on pay as it became overshadowed by wider disputes over government pay policies and public expenditure cuts and, on the teachers' side, by non-Burnham militancy or inter-union disputes. Controlling the pay negotiations centrally did not mean that consensus could be created nor the pay forum made effective. On the contrary. The shape of collective bargaining post-war had been increasingly dominated by central government pressures, intervention and regulation. Burnham contained a war of position around issues of control and the role of the unions (and later local government) in the education system.

In the quasi-market in education, post-1988, there is no real evidence of any change in this policy only in its strategic and tactical operation. The market in education raises the question of central control over teachers' pay in a more direct way than hitherto. The tensions in the reform between central regulation and supply and demand, seen in the National Curriculum and open enrolment, are not contradictory. The British way of governance, at its most efficient, used financial control, a simple regulatory framework and elite networks though the dominant metaphors or influences alter, their purpose remains intact, even in the 1990s. The leading edge of the required change at one time looked like the Grant-maintained sector and City Technology Colleges which are allowed experimental conditions to change; for example, they are not legally obliged to recognize teacher associations nor do they need to appoint or promote staff on the national conditions of service (Burgundy Book). However they may not have moved as fast in their ability to alter the industrial relations landscape as they were expected to do. Markets need strong regulation to operate effectively, for instance regulatory laws which stop the labour force intervening in the market by acting in combinations together. Teachers may only be in dispute with their own direct employers (under LMS, the governing body), may strike only with a secret ballot and may not engage lawfully in supporting colleagues elsewhere by engaging in dispute at their school. A restructuring of the workforce is going hand in hand with the change in the political economy of schools. Workforce flexibility is the shift government has encouraged; the trend is away from career development along salary scales (a consistent element of a Burnham tradition) and into discretionary payments by management (allowances are now called selective payments), which over the last few years, have become a larger and larger element of the overall pay bill. The education market needs strong central control to make certain that the conditions exist for it to work. The move to a pay review body is a policy shift consistent with the need for central control.

In this mode of control, the disciplining effect of the market (and the regularities of curriculum and testing controls) are offset by the lack of direct controls and the absence of an inclusive ideology, like partnership or professionalism. It is important to note that the constant return to the idea of central control, including central funding of teacher pay, by the Conservatives is significant as a further sign of the need to control directly.

The second element, of the regularities in the governing/managing of teachers, is the arrival of new forms of work in teaching; ways which will shape the union as well as its responses. Kerchner and Mitchell view the new unionism, a professional unionism, as reflecting the new school-based (or site) negotiating units and dealing with school productivity and quality. In this stage, two ideas have been introduced into teachers' work which are currently in operation in different kinds of manufacturing and service industries and are now represented in much new educational legislation in the West. These are the reorganization of work through human resource management (quality of working life/socio-technical change approaches) and the decentralization of school management and financing (Dankbaar, 1988; Van Huuten, 1987). Kerchner and Mitchell argue that teachers would work in 'functional work groups' (p. 254) that are integrated and cooperative (p. 237), experiment with 'new teaching technologies' (p. 255), 'deliver education' (p. 254) and carry out 'complete technical processes' (p. 254). Teachers would now be involved in school-level policy making on the 'purposes and character of educational programs' (p. 236) and they would take responsibility for their judgments and their work. To teachers, they will have a chance to develop their judgment and skill and shape school policy, a professional demand throughout teaching. Employers will have a flexibly organized, task-based workforce, constantly re-evaluating themselves and each other and be assessed on clear productivity targets. This is a vision of work that has been taken over from a shift in management practices known broadly as human resource management (Kochan *et al.*, 1986; Schein, 1987). Within this approach, which is built around the idea of reprofessionalizing work production (that is, making greater use of the 'flexibility, skills and tacit knowledge' of workers) and its strategic utilization to produce quality, there are variants but the general drift is clear. Workers must be involved in the production process and this can only be done by improving job satisfaction and allowing a form of industrial democracy. Behind the movement lies the influence of Japanese quality, mass production and the ideas it is based on. Briefly, although there are opportunities for workers in this system (as there would be for teachers), there are drawbacks. Employers want higher levels of quality production while workers wanted satisfaction and security but management has the last word and so, significantly for the idea of a new unionism, it is the unions which may suffer. No longer able to depend solely on 'us and them', the effectiveness of union bargaining is cut across and union leadership may be challenged if new work teams are seen as legitimate workplace representatives.

The decentralization of bargaining is another new development which is discussed in Kerchner and Mitchell but which is becoming common in the West. In a recent report on collective bargaining, the International Labour Office (ILO, 1989) made two important statements on the subject of decentralization, firstly:

> ... many employers are convinced that only enterprise-level bargaining can offer the flexibility needed in the organisation of production. (p. 8)

and secondly:

> ... (it has) given rise to the appearance of a whole series of often highly informal mechanisms of participation between employers and workers ... These (have) improved work organisation and productivity ... There have been attempts in some countries to impede the involvement of trade union representatives (...) in these participation experiences. (p. 21)

The report asks whether this represents a 'fundamental change' of attitudes in employment or a shift of power against the workers. In England, the conditions are right for a move to decentralized bargaining units following the institution of local financial management of schools, the suspension of national bargaining and the recent government decision to allow local enhanced salaries to compensate for skill or geographical teacher shortages. Teachers' work has been changing with some similarity to new industrial approaches; teachers are encouraged to see professionalism as a team-based quality in work, they have new contracts with discretionary elements and their schools are competing for pupils in a local market place.

What Place Do Teacher Unions Have in This New Landscape?

Teacher unions in England have always changed following the reorganization of the work (schooling), the new demands of members and the political and social context in which they operate. What changes are to be observed in the early 1990s? The first sign is an internal reorganization to meet the demands of these new conditions. All unions will have to adapt their organization in order to be able to respond to the reforms introduced by the 1988 Education Reform Act and by the changes in pay bargaining (caused by decentralized budgets and school governor influence). Although most schoolteacher unions have always had representatives based in individual schools, mainly to recruit new members, their role is likely to be enhanced by the introduction of local management of schools and the growth in the numbers of schools outside LEA control. For those unions whose membership has been almost entirely in the LEA sector, the move towards plant bargaining on many day-to-day issues will require some adjustment. Support for individual union members is likely to come increasingly from school representatives and paid union officials rather than from the elected officers of local associations based upon LEA boundaries. Two of the largest unions, the NUT and NAS/UWT, have decentralized union support regionally. Legal officers have been established in localities to service the new range of complaints. The NUT for example, following the election of a new general secretary (in the mid 1980s) and a policy called 'new realism', recognized the difficulties of national action and reorganized so that advice and counsel to its members, faced with an active school management, was readily accessible and so was decentralized to the regions. Its financial condition is such that a national action cannot be sustained, will probably be ineffective and will lose members. Making its services more effective for members is one option for the future. Direct mailing to members is more common as the LEA or local association stop acting as the centre of local union affairs. Members are more clearly than ever before consumers and look to the union for 'best buy'. As the identity of the unions, once located in clear sectoral or gendered areas, shifts so the differences between them may become less clear.

Either new identities will be created to attract or keep members or new levels of service (for example, cheap loans or mortgages). The very same problems that schools face in the market will face the unions — marketing, enrolment, staff quality, evaluation etc. Professional officers and their development are one aspect of this internal rationalization but so is the development of the association's key strengths, membership participation and elected officers. The union in a decentralized system will be as good as its local representative.

Another sign of change is the development of new policies to try to regain the educational leadership it lost in the last decades. As well as tactical interventions on the government's education policies which it has made, on the curriculum and on special educational needs, and the use of advertising and other means of influencing public opinions (such as a national billboard campaign on teacher shortages), the NUT is developing policy papers as a strategic response to government initiatives. The role of professional and public opinion is a key to this new realism, as is a long term vision of the changes it wishes to promote. A lot will depend on the strength of its own education programme in the union to inform members, training them in negotiating skills and developing commitment to new policies. It is probably easier to change if it is a gradual process and associations like AMMA which are still growing are at an advantage to one which has financial difficulties, like the NUT. A major boycott of the government's pupil testing programme in the early 1990s was extremely effective because it was based on inter-union collaboration.

Other kinds of unions, in industry or public services, faced with unemployment, declining revenue and loss of effectiveness, have merged. This has the effect of lowering costs, reducing overlap of services and eliminating inter-union conflict. Disunity between teacher unions weakens them all as they are competing against each other. NUT members at their annual conference have repeatedly demanded that their executive engages in unity discussions with other unions; this usually meant the NASUWT (which, because of their past history would be extremely difficult) and if a 'new realism' takes hold it could mean the more 'moderate' ATL (the Association of Teachers and Lecturers). The ATL and the smaller PAT (Professional Association of Teachers) discussed the creation of a new association and voted on a merger in 1991; this merger would have had to overcome the PAT's identity, founded on a principle of 'no-strike' action and the ATL tradition of not receiving head teachers into membership. This merger had been described by Peter Davison, PAT general secretary, as 'the force of the moderate majority' (*Education* 10.5.1991) and by Peter Smith, ATL general secretary as a genuinely democratic union. The merger failed to proceed. The Pay Review body, which has had a cautious but welcoming reception, in various degrees, from AMMA, PAT and the NASUWT might have created a unity from what can only be described as opposites but it only revealed the radical changes in the landscape. The old touchstone of disunity, 'for or against strike action', lost its strength when collective bargaining was politically removed. What will be the new touchstone?

Possible futures include

- increasingly nominal membership of unions for insurance purposes and other benefits. Indeed the 'benefits' may decide membership.
- the growth and coalition of unions with a supervisory membership (heads, deputies and then allowance holders etc.) A differentiated workforce might need differentiated unions.
- the move to non-unionism by a fragmented, semi-casual or low paid underclass of teachers and/or a revival of deep seated unionism, following their exclusion from market benefits.
- the identification with unions according to their policy objectives in a field where their tactical collective bargaining skills are redundant. Unions will move clearly into curriculum and other policies to retain and win members and develop their new identities.

Some of these possibilities seem contradictory and yet they may be exclusive but parallel options. It is unclear what function a teacher's association has without collective bargaining. Second guessing based on an earlier period where an educational market existed, the first fifty years approximately of a state sector (1870–1920), suggest the following:

- that many teachers lose in the market — women teachers in particular; teachers in regions with plentiful supply; older teachers.
- that organizing teachers varies in success — extremely difficult in rural/town areas but better in cities or larger city-based authorities.
- that sectoral division divide teachers who might have similar interests and that unions grow by appealing to and recruiting from teachers with sectoral interests — i.e., men/women teachers; primary/secondary teachers; class teachers/post holders/head teachers; selective and non-selective schools etc.

Only by a massive cultural shift inside the NUT in the first post-war period (approximately 1917–20) was it possible for many members to recognize that the unskilled needed to be in the same union as the skilled to defend a good standard of living. Today, competition and division appear to be stronger than unity. The creation of new kinds of teachers and the increasing tensions caused by school-based inter-teacher rivalries are likely to continue that trend, as indeed they are intended to do, unless another major shift in union attitudes can take place, of which merger talks might be an example.

The third area of reorganization (following internal restructuring and merger) might be the creation of a new General Teaching Council. The Labour Party has suggested that a new General Teaching Council might be responsible for the registration and discipline of teachers, regulation of entry into the profession and maintenance of professional standards. A Parliamentary Select Committee suggested that it could provide a forum for a greater unity between teacher and the Government. This would be the third GTC this century in England. Looking back, GTCs don't appear to have a useful function in relation to the tensions of the market and control over entry into teaching with one exception. They can act as a 'non-political' or dispute-free forum for discussion about rather idealistic versions of professionalism. The creation of this forum puts pressure on unions who wish to act as agencies for professional purpose and identity. On the other hand, if collective bargaining is removed what function might be left to the unions but to be advisory, both to members and to policy makers, and to live with the fact that advice in the market might not be needed.

Ways Out

If the old certainties about the work and value of teacher unions have been eroded, their past suggests that they will create a new role for themselves. The first English teacher union, the NUT, was shaped by, and influential in, the rise and growth of the modernist (colonialist and corporate modes of control) time in education, even more than it may recognize. The gradual inclusion of other unions, due to their growth in membership and the expansion of the state sector, was still configured by the idea and structures of the time. Key factors in teacher unionism — work homologies, control, membership, contradiction, context, identity, competition and work organization — will still remain as processes and issues.

But the problems of the market are severe as they attack the foundations of the unions, to serve and protect their members. A new role for the unions cannot exclude the difficulties they face by naively borrowing from new managerial thinking or creating a role which bears no relation to their purpose. The new decentralization of education in England had as one of its aims to break the power of professionals and the corporate management of education. To produce a glorious standard of professional unionism for the unions and ask them to fall in line behind it is not realistic in England. On the other hand, a renewed militancy to safeguard conditions of work is also not realistic. In the union's favour at the moment is a shortage of teachers, they are not being recruited nor are they being retained. In a seller's market, power should move to the teachers; this has happened at significant periods in the past.

A 'pragmatic' course of action would include a renewed strategic argument for a public service professionalism combined with effective local union organization. The pragmatic course would search for allies in education with other unions and with major education providers. The latter would include cities searching for improvements in their education services; they would be looking for local associations to negotiate with their local authorities, guaranteeing value in exchange for higher investment. Although these cities exist, within the Learning Cities network, the move to new conditions of work has not yet allowed a reciprocal movement within the teacher unions to emerge. If it did then this would begin to look like the USA reform movement, described by Kerchner and Mitchell.

In a system controlled by strong managerialism, regulation and cost-cutting, a campaign based on professionalism in public service might be effective politically (this would be part of what Michael Barber called 'strategic unionism' (Barber, 1992)). An expression of public service values and a guarantee of public accountability is probably the next effective political step for some of the unions. Professional unionism would be the managerial response that a new Labour Government would prefer. It would demand from Labour the creation of a new professional discourse so that, while the Conservative reforms of education remain substantially intact, a negotiated agreement about resources, accountability and outcomes can take place between 'partners'.

11 Orderings and Disorderings: Questions About the Work of the Primary Head in the New Public/Private Mix

The changes to primary schools, associated with the rise of the quasi-market and the decline of the public service in education, and the meaning of these changes, are difficult to ascertain. This is due to the lack of information about the workings of state schools in previous decades, indeed this is one of the issues at the centre of this book. There is no difficulty reading about what schools should be doing at any time but there is a problem in finding out what they did do. The intended and unintended consequences of a shift into a quasi-market based education system have configured educational research responses to the reforms of the late 1980s but one of the main difficulties in researching this area is the lack of comparative data.

This paper is drawn from a study of a particular school, a suburban junior school with about 350 pubils, situated in a large urban conurbation in England. It concentrates on the way the head teachers see this school, in the 1970s and in the mid-1990s, and is based upon a reading of the school logbook and a series of interviews made with its head in 1994 and 1995. The paper will try to compare the same primary school in the public service and in the public/private service of the quasi-market, in different decades; the 1970s represent firstly, a period when the post-war consensus around the Government of the education system was gradually changing but the administration of that system remained substantially intact, and secondly, the 1990s represent a period when a new form of government and administration was settling down.

One problem with comparisons is that they may lack a grasp of substantive, rather than surface or rhetorical, realities. This bedevilled earlier comparative statements about the shift from autonomy and professionalism to control in teaching, for example, as the result of the 1988 Act. It obscures comparative analyses which try to describe improvements or regressive processes in teaching skills, pedagogy and classrooms.[1] This paper compares two texts produced by three heads of the same primary school; two wrote in the 1970s and one was interviewed in the mid-1990s.[2] It views the situation of their work from their point of view (although it is recognized that this has to be surmised and their purposes and audiences were different). The school logbook is an official diary, exclusive to the head, who is the only one with the power to write it but who has to produce it for more powerful outsiders (Inspectors etc.).

By drawing upon recent work on the sociology of organizations and identity to discuss their ordering of work and the comparisons between the school in the two periods (Law, 1994; Hall, 1992) this paper will try to conceptualize the shifts or changes in the school, described and inscribed by the heads, by using a conceptual framework, modes of ordering (Law, 1994), to describe the patterning of work and its social relations by organizational narratives. Modes of ordering contain descriptions of working, serve as explanations of working and embody place and structure. They are ways of describing work and physical presences in it. The mode of ordering will be used to illuminate the positionality of the head teachers and the way in which the demands of the public service or market shaped or shape their organizational narrative and ordering of work. The school logbook entries are not read here as a commonsense quotidian narrative but as a way of seeing the work of the school, an organizational narrative which orders the school, its spaces and its personnel. The head teacher interviews were based on the same kind of entries (and their meanings) that had been made by earlier head teachers. The school in question has remained physically the same since its creation and furbishment in the early 1950s and its physical layout of the school and its furniture still determine what is possible in the routines of the school. However, the mode of ordering of the school reflects more than commonsense routines, it orders the way people work, their understanding of what it is and who does it. It configures the work relations of the school. Routines of work are embedded in socially located ideas about the school, its teachers and its purposes. Changes in the mode of ordering of the primary school will be analysed to explore the significance of the public service and quasi market periods in which the school existed and to make a judgment about the substantive and not merely superficial changes which have occurred in the school.

The School in the 1970s

The case school organizational narrative in the 1970s was written by two heads in the daily school logbook, a form of professional diary. It is a way of patterning work and of structuring it. Work is seen through the ideas of presence, absence and space principally. The logbook contains a dizzying list of entries and exits by teachers. The impression is given that their presence is all that was required; that is, a class had to be taken but the purpose of the 'taking' is obscured. Coping with emergency exits by teachers are as preoccupying as managing a known exit in advance. Somebody has to be with the children. Information about teachers has to be inferred. It reflects the head's preoccupation with making sure the children are in class and there is an adult with them: the problem of containing children is expressed through descriptions partial or whole school closures. Snow, gas leaks and heating problems feature as major events mainly because of the exclusion of children from an hour to a week. The logbook expresses, in a fairly rational and abrupt way, the head's overriding concern with defining work and keeping it ordered. It is working if there are teachers in all the classes with their children and not working properly if children are unsupervised or excluded by teacher absence or structural emergency. Work can be viewed through the use and non-use of space: in the head's patterning of work, the classroom is a workplace and is dependent on all other school spaces being clear of pupils and teachers. The staffroom space had no work function and the head's room is the space from which all others are ordered.

Another idea used in describing their work is number. The number of children, of classes and of teachers is threaded throughout and becomes the subtext of work. At the beginning of every year, the number of pupils is noted, a list of teachers and their classes is made and those teachers without classes (supernumeraries) are listed with an explanation of their mobile work pattern. Yet while the crucial nature of the teacher/class relation is reported regularly, only presence, absence, space and number seem to define the patterning of work.

In the mid-1970s, a new form of patterning develops. Arranging teachers became more visible; it began to shift from arranging by their class age group and into grading by new, special posts (described as responsibilities). In 1973, for example, sixteen teachers worked in the school and nine of them had scale post responsibilities; that is, they had additional payments, on a rising scale, to take on additional (i.e., schoolwide not class-based) tasks. These responsibilities are not described and may have been a reward for seniority or gendered role or scarcity.

Arranging teachers reflected a prioritizing by the head (with the LEA Officer's permission) of the curriculum areas and teachers in the school. It is the first time they reach visibility in the account. The highest scale was given to a teacher who had been with the school since 1954, regularly took the top A-stream class and specialized in music. Since music was a feature of the annual parents' evening and other concerts, involved a school band (of varying sizes) and was regularly praised by the head, the Scale 4 award seems logical (Scale posts ran from the lowest point (1) to the highest (4) in this scale). Needlework had a Sc 3 post attached to it: this area was sometimes supported by two part-time teaching assistants and so was a prominent feature of the curriculum. The School Annexe is separated from the junior school by a walk of approximately forty yards and consists of several classrooms and a single year group: it had a Scale 3 post for the teacher in charge. This new patterning of work reflected a preference made by the head into new structures and relations of work. It was variable, single reward given, without other information, on the basis of presence and absence. No other statement about the substantive nature of the scale posts, and how they worked was made. Not until the end of the decade did the head log that he had discussed new areas of 'responsibility' with all members of staff without explaining the need to do so or the content of the discussions. Not until the following decade is there any mention of staff meetings. The looseness of the scale descriptions, their connectedness/disconnectedness from the 'areas of responsibility' and their arbitrary grading and arrival/disappearance suggest a system that was new to the head's ordering of work in the school.

The boundaries between the school and the outside world are well defined in this period. The head left the school every year and went to a day meeting of local schools which involved an Education Authority Officer, usually the Chief Education Officer. Inspectors came in to inspect different aspects of their work and talk to the teachers. No teacher left the school to attend professional training until a day in 1977 and then again in 1978 a teacher went out and that was that until the early 1980s. The knowledge base of the teachers has to be surmised from their training. They had no in-service programme available to them or access to local inset. There is a great silence about their skills, curriculum knowledge and most of all, classroom life. What they know may come from within the school, for example, by discussion or by reflection on practical experience or is imported privately through family or friends. The work is confining, it is physically bounded and the exit and entry points are overseen. In this mode of ordering, the silence about their work appears to be intentional. It may be a reflection of a dualism in which the head represents the significant, rational ordering of thought in the school and the teachers represent the labourers fulfilling that ordering.

The school can be seen as quiescent and compliant. It orders itself while waiting for the LEA to decide what it needs to do. It may try to prompt the LEA but the Logbook only once shows irritation with the lack of LEA support and this was when the acting head, in the late 1970s, underlined the fact that it took ten weeks to get a roof repaired. Usually the school waits. It waits for the ByeLaws Officer, the Divisional Administrative Assistant, the Head of Supplies, the Caretakers section and City Engineers. It waits for the Inspector to come, to observe and to propose or confirm. It has to perfect arguments to convince a centralized bureaucracy that a new floor polishing machine is vital or there is a gas leak or there are no secure cupboards. It waits for an inspector to call and close classrooms that are impossibly cold and which make the children and the teachers ill. The collected correspondence on the new curtains for the hall and the time spent placating, consulting and waiting for decisions outweighs most other single events, including successful curriculum topics and music shows. Inspectors call and promote social studies or environmental studies or invite (demand) their involvement in major children's exhibitions or some engagement in city twinning. Teachers appear redeployed from elsewhere, almost without notice. (The view of the patterning of work in the school available within the logbook is partial, of course, and limited by the nature of the document itself. This does not affect the argument about the patterning of work though it limits its range).

The key words which I have used to analyse this organizational narrative of the school are presence, absence, space, grading, confining, quiescence and compliance. While these modes of ordering to describe the patterning of work and its social relations are seen through this organizational narrative, they are embodied in place and structure. Although they are seen here in the logbook as expressed by heads, I intend to view them as partially constructed by the nature of the school context in the 1970s, that is, they are reflections or effects of the public school system at the time. For the school in question, this meant the city Local Education Authority visible in the correspondence about elements of the school, such as its staffing or new curtains, or its opening or closure; or in the visits of its officials, such as engineers or inspectors. The latter would command, intervene, inform or agree the work of the school.

Whatever else the school in the public service may be configured by (such as government policies or restated public and media accounts of service in education), one version of its ordering of the social relations of work in the primary school in a period of public service hegemony gives the following conclusion. The school appears to order itself through a significant person, the head, and through the actions of the city authority. Significant ordering occurs around the quantifiable and visible aspects of the school (teacher and pupil numbers and spaces) and not around qualitative and invisible aspects (such as learning, development, change or classrooms). Significant internal and external ordering occurs as an effect of the power relations which construct the school as confined and compliant.

The School in the 1990s

Presence and absence from school are still demonstrated in the explanations of the head but they may pattern work in different ways. Teacher presence is felt through more than quantitative information, it surfaces through the regular reference to costs. The presence or not of the teacher is a cost. If present, other costs of supply teaching do not occur. There is still a concern for absence and presence but this has altered meaning. The rule of cost has made visible to all the entrances and exits of pupils and staff as it has overturned the silence about curriculum, teaching and staffrooms. Cost is a new subtext and connects a number of factors in a new unity. Presence is not just an issue for the head's patterning of work, it is visible in the behaviours of teachers: they plan their absences for hospital operations to avoid difficulties months in advance, they resist absence even when medically advised to do so. The lack of pupils means a threat of permanent absence for some teachers; they no longer recruit well, for complex reasons, from the local infant school and so have created a nursery unit to help the infant school recruit. The loss of income from the decline in pupil entry means teacher redundancy somewhere down the line. The disciplinary effect of the market has significantly affected the ordering of work as absence means costs which changes social relations.

Presence works in other ways. Presence in the school does not just mean in the classroom but in the team and in the leading of a curriculum area. Supply teachers take a class but not the management role of the curriculum leader. Presence is necessary for the regular meetings about the short- and long-term planning of the new, differentiated and specialized curriculum, across a year, in a phase team. It is necessary for the weekly meetings for production and review of planning and policy documents and for the termly day-long staff meetings. The presence of the teachers is felt in the systems file of the school, which is produced by them (and the head) in thick documentation on school management and curriculum policy and procedures. It is also felt in the development plan of the school in which their named presence is followed by their targets, success criteria, resources, school funding and evaluation strategies. It is recognized in the curriculum file in every classroom in which all school curriculum policies are collected. The planning activity of the school links all the visible presences together and embodies their occupation of a space from which they were excluded. Their presence in the classroom is no longer so obscured.

The silence about the spaces the teachers inhabited in the 1970s and the invisibility of the classroom and the curriculum has been replaced by a considerable tumult and activity. This is closely related to the externally derived mode of ordering of the National Curriculum, which in turn has been incorporated into key planning documents (like the annual School Development Plan) and in a form which can be externally inspected by local authority inspectors, school governors and the inspectors of the Office for Standards in Education. The earlier grading of teachers by posts of responsibility has been transformed, by a sequence of moves into curriculum leadership posts, based on qualification or aptitude or amenability, and have professional development, monitoring and evaluation duties attached to them. A consequence of this transformation is the way school boundaries, once so confining, have been altered. Forty separate training courses had been taken by the school teachers since 1988 and in 1994 fifteen one or two day courses were taken. Each of the courses were about some aspect of the curriculum leader's role or were used to bring new skills into the school and had to be reported back at a staff meeting and a report produced for the system file. National reports are dissected by teams, leaders and in meetings. A recent inspectors's report on the school has continued this outside patterning of work by asking for an action plan which would allow curriculum leaders to monitor other classroom teachers more closely, observe them teaching and evaluate them. Not only the head but the school secretary or administrative officer leave the school regularly to share information freely with other schools about to undergo Ofsted inspection; they enter the schools to talk to the teachers and the support staff and they take with them a great deal of information about finance, planning and teaching. The organizational narrative of the head makes constant reference to outside school agencies and agents.

The boundaries of work have a new patterning derived from the complexity of the education and employment regulations in the intervening period. Relations with local inspectors and officials of the local education authority continue although they have shifted as costing mechanisms and altered city powers have created new social relations between them. For example, the pupil admissions were determined by the floor space of the school which had to be officially measured. The head found a city official measuring part of the school early in the morning and invited him to leave. He found his intrusion, once legitimate in the quiescent school, inappropriate; it did not recognize the shift in power to the school. The official should have entered with permission.

The complexity of the work situation has altered in other ways. There are new groups of people working in school. The LEA recognizes at least fourteen categories of support staff working in school (such as classroom assistants, lunch supervisors, school bursars, welfare and integration assistants, pre-school workers etc.) and the school has several new groups of workers within it, compared to the 1970s. Each of these employees has a job description and conditions of employment. (All these staff will be inspected by the Ofsted inspectors.) Even when there is a continuation of a post, such as the school secretary, the work has altered considerably. Budgets, financial planning and computerized systems have changed the office of the secretary. The secretary checks all invoices and spends a lot of time in communication with suppliers or city officials about the cost, the timing and the quality of services to the school. The school does not act as a compliant receiver but as an active agent; it acts as a purchaser as well as a provider. Again, the school appears to order itself through a significant person, the head. Significant ordering occurs around the quantifiable and visible aspects of the school, especially through costs, and around qualitative and newly, visible aspects, such as curriculum planning. Significant internal and external ordering occurs as an effect of the power relations which construct the school as open and responsible.

Ordering and Disordering: The Public/Private Mix

Modes of ordering pattern work through the organizational narratives and explanations which are embodied in work and reshaped by it. A mode of ordering in the primary school, seen within the organizational narratives of the headteachers, has consistencies drawn from the practical needs of the site (safety, logistics, size etc.) and ideological assumptions about the social relations of work (power, task, space, teacher etc.) within it. Work, in this ordering, has two main properties, existing in the same statements: it is both a commonsense ordering of tasks, space and people and it is a patterning of work drawn from or an effect of social and political ideas *about* work. Although expressed within commonsense and natural statements which shape work and its significant features, it is also a vehicle for specific social ideas about what is commonsense and natural in work. Returning to the 1970s and a particular mode of ordering reveals the unnatural aspects of the social relations of work and how this is manifested in the encounters, structures and spaces of school. Compliance and absence were key aspects of this period, once perfectly congruent with work, now uneasily inappropriate when compared to the 1990s. The visibilities of work in the 1990s comprise a new patterning in which the organizational narratives about teaching have revealed their work within the school and to outsiders. This recognition of responsibility and skill breaks the confines of the older narrative but also opens up the teacher to new and further patterning.

The tight organizational narrative of work in the primary school produced by the current head and the teacher is determined in two ways; by the high level of specification demanded of its curriculum, planning and evaluation and the discipline of its financial controls. These specifications and controls are also visible and embodied in the structures and commodities of the school. Descriptions and explanations about the school operate as a new commonsense about work in which the language of costs, management, personnel, planning and assessment are all threaded through. This 1990s head's mode of ordering is congruent with much of these changes and to the new commonsense narrative of meaning of work in the school. This is not to say that there is a harmony in the daily organizational narratives of work: it is precarious, complex, risky, intense etc. But it is the social and political patterning of work in this mode of ordering which contains problems of value which disrupt work and produce a disordering of it.

Costs are not just a ruler applied to action within the school but to the suppliers of goods and services to it. When the school needs painting, for example, then estimates are compared and time and quality taken into account. The head wants value for money. However, many transactions are not so clear cut, especially when they apply to educational services. It is very hard to deduce the boundaries within service relations between public and commercial or private worlds. Advice merges into consultancy or sales. The ambiguities of conversations about many aspects of the school as a business disorder this head's work and are a direct consequence of the new quasi-market.

I want to take several examples of this disordering aspect to work. Educational psychologists have been working as a city-wide service for many years. They may not have been regular visitors or supporters to some schools but they were an available service for them, in theory. The same psychologist who worked with the school in the past, sharing advice or working with the teacher on a problem, will arrive today. This time his support for the school will offer a limited free service and yet at some unspecified point in the conversation may begin to consider charging for his time and may offer the school more extended advice but with a consultancy fee attached. The difficulties for the head are extended throughout this new patterning of work: will this person begin to charge? is this a free service offered by an old friend? As the head describes the problem, 'this person comes with a cost' (Project Notes 17 October 1995).

Secondly, several classes were engaged in an interesting project on space exploration. They were trialling materials for an exciting project, linked to schools across Britain and to the USA; they enjoyed it and the teachers worked hard on it to make it work. The project arrived at the school by means of a personal invitation, given by ex-local education staff, at a meeting of a regular network of primary heads. The merits of the project begin to diminish as it appeared badly organized but the real crunch came when it appeared that the project was 'part of a commercial undertaking', the head became concerned that the school was being used as part of a 'promotion exercise' and withdrew it from the project. Looking back, the head suggested that the problem came because the project entered the school through a public service network, (the primary heads meeting) and through the public service reputations of the promoters. Without those two aspects of entry, it is unlikely he would have wanted the school involved. He was concerned about their back door entry into the school and their commercial purpose.

Thirdly, the head has had regular involvement in a particular cross-curricula area. A special curriculum support unit for this area has operated in the city for several years. It is partly paid for by a central charge made upon all schools, through monies retained by the centre. The unit has to raise its own money to supplement its income and retain jobs. Questions about the funding of the unit and the services it provides for schools raised further questions about its fees, the extent of its 'free' services and the flexibility of its subscriptions. In a discussion about these issues with the unit leader, the latter used the phrase 'it's all part of the family of . . .' This stimulated the head to wonder about the variations in services, costs and personnel that were oper-ating in the city and the problem of trying to reunite in education those things that were now torn apart. The idea of the 'family' no longer worked to unite variations in the public service and the problems of the social relations of education.

The final example is drawn from the consistent bidding for additional resources which occupies the head. While costs, especially salary costs, are fixed and demands upon income rises, the need to raise income is extremely important. (NAHT Survey 1994 — Heads use a wide range of activities to boost school income, paying for 'bread and butter materials' with 'entrepreneurial activities', p. 17). Every opportunity to increase income is taken by the head of this school; bids were made to charities, education–business partnerships, LEA special projects, in-service courses, Arts and Technology Councils in 1994–5. 'Making the case' for extra resource is vital and 'you have to go looking for things' (Notes 7 March). A successful bid is important to the school and sat-isfying to the head but it is also a point of contradiction for the head. A successful bid means that other schools, whose needs may be greater, he feels, lose out.

The problems the head reveals, in these examples, are to do with the less easily discernible aspects of the patterning of work and its new social rela-tions. It is not the problems of the practical needs of the site but the problems of the social relations of work, produced by the introduction of the market into the public service customs of work. It does not exist as a procedural error in accounting or an inadequate curriculum plan or an unsatisfactory management structure or fear of Ofsted inspections. These are all daily or annual problems but can be managed. It is a problem of the patterning of work drawn from or an effect of social and political ideas about work. It exists within the moral and political facets of the mode of ordering of the head and creates a form of disordering. The head splits the new ordering activity of work from a part of its meaning. He expects people to behave within the older public ideas about service. While the head's ordering of schools uses, with relative ease, the specification demanded of its curriculum, planning and evaluation procedures and the discipline of its financial controls, it is disordered by the shift away form public service social relations of work.

The consequences of working in a changed situation in schools have been discussed in a number of ways in English research, from the idea of upskilling, to teacher differentiation and flexibility, to multiple innovation and workload studies. Another way is through the idea of the moral economy of the schools, a way in which different forms of value statements, apparently contradictory, were used, by heads, to describe the new entrepreneurship and marketing activities in their work (Ball, 1994). The point I wish to make is that work is produced within a mode of ordering which contains particular organizational narratives which are incorporated and symbolized within the site of educational work. The mode of ordering describes the practical aspects of the organizing *of* the site and ideological assumptions about the social relations of work *at* the site; the former describes the shift of work into new patterns and the latter involves embedded political and social explanations and judgments about the nature and relations of work. The analysis of upskilling in work *and* the moral discourses about work exist within the same space, the mode of ordering work.

Review

The school appears within a mode of ordering created at different times and in different ways. The commonsense ideas about the practicalities, the patternings and the social relations of work, have similarities and differences across the decades. The visibility of teaching, curriculum and assessment, the heightening of grading and the reduction of the confining and boundaried aspects of school are examples of difference between the 1970s and the 1990s. The new managerialism pervades the new organizational narrative of the school and has opened it up for inspection. The difference between the two main organizational narratives reveals the way in which descriptions of school work hide their social and ideological features within a commonsense language of work. However, while there are differences between the two main organizational narratives, are those differences indicative of public service and of quasi-market work? It is easier to see the way in which the complexities and visibilities of work today have been constructed by organizational narratives tightly constrained by the external impacts of the quasi-market. What is not so clear is the social embeddedness of public service ideas within the earlier work.

Primary teachers, seen within the logbook, are described only by means of presence and their work is silent and classroom contained. It seems incongruous to relate the idea of compliance or of invisibility to public service work yet, in this school at that time, they were homologous. When it is used within the explanations of the current head, public service stands for a way of collectively relating to others in education without commerce and within a common moral and educational framework. (Public service could mean other things, for example, professional control, but with this head, it is used in this specific manner.)

In addition to the ordering of work there is a new sense of disordering. Willing to be entrepreneurial but not commercial, the head's mode of ordering demands visibility and initiative but is disordered by new trading relations appearing in the social relations of work. This disordering is centred upon certain kinds of service relations in work; his identity, in Mercer's words, is at issue in this situation

> when something assumed to be fixed, coherent and stable is displaced by the experience of doubt and uncertainty. (Mercer, 1990)

Aspects of the market in his work have not become embedded nor have they forged a new identity or mode of ordering. Instead they cause a disordering in his organizational narrative. Not the practice but the idea of an imagined community of public service rules his actions even though it appears that he is a successful head in the quasi-market, ordering the entrepreneurial school. It appears to be a paradox that the effect of the quasi-market appears to have heightened the ordering of work by the head and yet partially disordered him by the promotion of commercial relations.

Note

1 Recent examples in England of published accounts making statements about the intensification or proletarianization or upskilling of teaching are now numerous. Likely inferences from comparative material are used against quantitative data or sometimes just panglossian assertion. Ways of deepening the analysis of changes to work, taken over time, are still to be encouraged.
2 The first part of the logbook was written by a Head from the start of the school in 1954 to his retirement in 1973; the second one retired in 1984; the last Head began in 1984.

Conclusion: A Synthetic Exit

The modern period in education was about the macro, the grand narrative of the modernizing of mass education, with the illuminating and obscuring representations of partnership and professionalism. It consistently drew attention to its uniqueness and difference, formed against European traditions and drawing upon the way of an 'English' democracy in its government and images. The need to manage a modernization programme, which created a mass of people (teachers) who could undermine it and a state which devised it, strengthened a sophisticated narrative in which indirect controls and powerful images were the principal forms. The value of this approach lay in the fact that it 'worked with the grain' of social aspiration and reform and was constructed and managed at a distance, leaving room for incremental change and local difference. It produced a notion of public which was also one of mass.

It has been replaced by the micro, the local and institutional report, the minor geographies of space and locality. The school is now the franchised agency, looking entirely into itself, no longer concerned with its place in *a* system, it is now *the* system. There is only the micro. The absence of regional or national representations has been replaced by the globalization of vision in a language of improvement and quality shared by education in many countries and with other forms of work.

The changes of the last few years have been driven by the marketization and restructuring of education. These changes have reshaped teaching. It is arguable whether teachers have become upskilled by the new curriculum, its planning and assessment although it is clear that a whole new group of semi-skilled teachers, the classroom assistants, have been created in significant numbers. Intensification of work through a lengthening of the hours of work and the range and duties within it has resulted from the creation of new devolved responsibilities within the education system. A teacher's pedagogy and content will need to be regularly updated to ensure improvement in the substantive and process areas of the curriculum. Updating will occur through centralized, regular guidelines on the curriculum, inspection reports and flexible procedures within the school for inset. At the same time as work has changed it has become more transparent; it is open to other teachers, head teachers, inspectors and most of all, to government. Assessment of pupils has been followed by teacher assessment; even a decision about classroom layout, rows or groups, can become a question of governmental comment and debate in relation to performance indicators and output levels. Teachers appear to be developing new skills in pedagogy and assessment, new subject expertise, specialist functions of supervision over staff, teamworking, new job descriptions and a developmental planning process in the school.

The break with the past can be seen in the material conditions circumscribing the political relations between teachers and their employers. Collective pay bargaining, through the central Burnham panel, was withdrawn and replaced by a pay review body and local pay flexibilities. The breaking down of the settled order of the post-war education system, built on national agreement and local education authority policy, has resulted in new labour markets in teaching. A local market is created through levels of income generation, locality and governor autonomies over pay. Performance, productivity and reward will be the key words now, replacing service, scale and duty.

The devolving of responsibility to the teacher appears to have created the very responsibility they were supposed to have in the modern period. Of course, the context is very different. The loose talk about power and autonomy has gone, they are no longer the responsible experts of modernization, needed to manage mass schooling, but the supervised employee. Choice and diversity applies to teachers if it applies to schools and a single containing myth to describe teachers in a public service is no longer possible. Differentiated teachers is the result. What they have in common is the job requirement, to be a willing, flexible operative, assessing and being assessed. They are employed in a situation where they no longer leave the 'visible' spaces of the school for the private work of the classroom, everywhere is visible and so controllable. As the sensitivity of their work has grown, in public debate and with local parents and communities, so their openness to observation has increased. The new policy context in primary education has focused clearly upon the teaching skills, methods and organization of work in primary schools. It works in quite the opposite way to the earlier period; the details of work are expressed as public debate or turned into quick fixes, not left alone and managed at a distance. A recent debate about time for homework is one example. Responsibility as partners in the service has been replaced by direct responsibility for productivity and results. The public spaces in which they exerted power, often in hostile circumstance, has been reduced to the boundaries of the school. Yet it is not at all clear what kind of power teachers had at school and in education in the past. What they had was the power of the modernizing and very 'English' discourse behind them, in which they were placed and which reflected well upon them if they did not contest or disrupt it. The stability of the whole professional discourse has been replaced by the built in instability of the constant restructuring of the transparent elements of their work.

The greatest change has been in the lack of the modernizing vision particularly to the purpose and value of education, indeed the very opposite is felt to be the case. Teachers feel vilified by government and its agencies, there is no vision only failure. The collapse of the modern project of the mass education system and the retreat of the State from its promotion has left teachers with the blame for its failure. This is coupled with a suspicion of teachers, as a professional group, who may act, in concert, to interfere in the market. This suspicion is legitimate as the influence of social movements on teachers are probably still at work, opening them to arguments about anti-racism, inequality, single issue politics etc. Without a modernizing vision which can be colonized by teachers this seems unlikely to be effective. The immediate future appears to be signified by key words like regulation and improvement which lack the sense of purpose of the past, however flawed or cynical it was. Energizing teachers has been replaced by scrutinizing them, or better still occupying them with self scrutiny.

Teachers' work is defined by the social and political policies of the particular time, it is never a question of defining technical skills alone. Although there were developing and distinctive demands upon teachers in the past, the significance of the present lies in the restructuring and reshaping of teachers' work to fit into a redesign of the education system into different sectors and fragmented sites. The question 'what is the teacher's job?' today is a practical question and a theoretical question; the key issues are focused upon the conceptualization of skill, professionalism, work relations and work cultures, within the biographical and school settings and mediated within the local and national policy contexts.

No system is impermeable. The labour market, skills, organizational plans and goals of the new local education system might be capable of disciplining and shaping the teacher but the social, economic and political conditions in which the teacher and the school exist will create the same contradictions and tensions as the modern period did. Unions are searching for a role, schools are cooperating together and the disciplining of the teacher by inspection continues. The search for a new version of the public in schools will not be left to the micro settings in which it exists nor to the superficialities of party agenda.

Bibliography

ABCA (1942) *The A.B.C.A. Handbook* (Middle East edn, 3 vols.) London, ABCA.

ABCA (1943) *The Story of the Army Bureau of Current Affairs* (film), London, Ministry of Information.

ABCA (1945a) *Public Opinion 1945* (film), London, Central Office of Information.

ABCA (1945b) *Town and Country Planning 1945* (film), London, Central Office of Information.

ALEXANDER, W. (1954) *Education in England and How it Works*, Newnes.

ALLEN, J. (1993) 'Post-industrialism and post-fordism', in HALL, S., HELD, D. and McGREW, T. (Eds) *Modernity and its Futures*, Cambridge, Polity Press.

APPLE, M. (1990) *Teachers and Texts*, London, Routledge.

ASTMS REPORT (1987) *Quality Circles*, London, ASTMS.

AUDIT COMMISSION (1991) *Management within Primary Schools*, London, HMSO.

BAGGULEY, P. (1992) 'Social change, the middle class and the emergence of "new social movements": A critical analysis,' *Sociological Review*, pp. 26–48.

BALL, S. (1990) *Markets, Morality and Equality in Education*, London, Tufnell Press.

BALL, S. (1994) *Education Reform*, Milton Keynes, Open University Press.

BARBER, M. (1992) *Education and the Teacher Unions*, London, Cassell.

BARKER, R. (1972) *Education and Politics 1900–1951*, Clarendon Press.

BENN, C. and SIMON, B. (1970) *Half Way There*, Harmondsworth, Penguin.

BLISHEN, E. (1955) *Roaring Boys: A Schoolmaster's Agony*, London, Thames and Hudson.

BLISHEN, E. (1969) *This Right Soft Lot*, London, Thames and Hudson.

BLUMER, H. (Ed) (1979) *Critique of Research in the Social Sciences: An Appraisal of Thomas and Znaniecki's The Polish Peasant in Europe and America*, New Jersey, Transaction Books.

BOARD OF EDUCATION (1907) *Circular 573 Memorandum on the History and Prospects of the Pupil–Teacher System*, London, HMSO.

BRAITHWAITE, E.R. (1959) *To Sir, With Love*, London, Bodley Head.

BUSHER, H. and SARAN, R. (1992) *Teachers' Conditions of Employment*, London, Kogan Page.

CALDER, A. (Ed) (1982) *The People's War in Britain 1939–1945*, London, Granada.

CAMPBELL, R.J., EVANS, L., ST J. NEILL, S.R. and PACKWOOD, A. (1991) 'The use and management of infant teachers' time', Policy Analysis Unit Seminar Paper, University of Warwick.

CCCS (1981) *Unpopular Education*, London, Hutchinson.

CENTRAL ADVISORY COUNCIL FOR EDUCATION (1963) *Half our Future* (The Newsom Report), London, HMSO.

CLARKE, F. (1940) *Education and Social Change*, London, Sheldon Press.

COLE, G.D.H. (1920a) *Chaos and Order in Industry*, London, Methuen.

COLE, G.D.H. (1920b) *Guild Socialism Restated*, London, Parsons.

CONS, G.J. and FLETCHER, C. (1938) *Actuality in the School*, London, Methuen.

COPELMAN, D.M. (1985) 'Women in the classroom struggle: Elementary school teachers in London 1870–1914', Princeton, PhD thesis.

CROWDER, M. (1968) *West Africa under Colonial Rule*, London, Hutchinson.

DANKBAAR, B. (1988) 'New production concepts, management strategies and the quality of work', in *Work, Employment and Society*, **2**, 1, pp. 25–50.

DARMANIN, M. (1985) 'Malta's teachers and social change', in LAWN, M. (Ed) *Politics of Teacher Unionism*, London, Croom Helm.

DENT, H. (1942) *A New Order in English Education*, London, University of London Press.

DENT, H. (1944) *Education in Transition: A Sociological Study of the Impact of War on English Education 1939–1943*, London, Kegan Paul.

DENT, H. (1949) *Secondary Education for All*, London, Routledge and Kegan Paul.

DENT, H. (1962) *The Training of Teachers in the United Kingdom*, London, Longmans.

DEPARTMENT OF EDUCATION AND SCIENCE (1985) *Better Schools*, London, HMSO.

DIRECTORATE OF ARMY Education (1944) *The British Way and Purpose* (consolidated edn, booklets 1–18), London, DAE.

DUCLAUD-WILLIAMS, R. (1985) 'Teacher unions and educational policy in France', in LAWN, M. (Ed) *The Politics of Teacher Unionism*, London, Croom Helm.

DRAY, J. and JORDAN, D. (1952) *A Handbook of Social Studies*, London, Methuen.

EDUCATION HANDBOOK No 3 (1948) *Partnerships in Education*, Norwich, Jarrold and Sons.

EDWARDS, B. (1974) *The Burston School Strike*, London, Lawrence and Wishart.

FENWICK, I.G.K. (1976) *The Comprehensive School 1944–1970*, London, Methuen.

FISHER, S. (1992) 'A lifetime of education reform', in *Education Review*, **6**, 1.

FLORIN, C. (1987) *Kampen om Katedern*, Umeå University, Sweden.

GOODSON, I. (1983) *School Subjects and Curriculum Change*, London, Croom Helm.

GOULBOURNE, H. (1988) *Teachers: Education and Politics in Jamaica 1892–1972*, London, Macmillan Caribbean.

GORDON, P. (1958) 'The handbook of suggestions for teachers: Its origins and evolution', in *Journal of Educational Administration and History*, **17**, 1, pp. 41–7.

GOSDEN, P.H.J.H. (1972) *The Evolution of a Profession*, Oxford Blackwell, p. 345.

GRACE, G. (1978) *Teachers, Ideology and Control*, London, Routledge and Kegan Paul.

HALL, S. (1989) 'The meaning of new times', in HALL, S. and JACQUES, M. (Eds) *New Times*, London, Lawrence and Wishart.

HALL, S. (1992) 'The question of cultural identity', in HALL, S., HELD, D. and McGREW, T. (Eds) *Modernity and its Futures*, Cambridge, Polity Press.

HALL, S. and JACQUES, M. (1989) *New Times*, London, Lawrence and Wishart.

HARBAJHAN SINGH BRAR (1988) 'Unequal opportunities: The recruitment, selection and promotion prospects for black teachers', in LAWN, M. and GRACE, G. (1988) *Teachers: The Culture and Politics of Work*, London, Falmer Press.

HMI (1985) *Education Observed 3 Good Teachers*, London, HMSO.

HMI (1992) *Non-teaching Staff in Schools*, London, HMSO.

HAWKINS, T.H. and BRIMBLE, L.J.F. (1947) *Adult Education: The Record of the British Army*, London, Macmillan.

HAYES, D. (1990) *Behind the Silicon Curtain: The Seductions of Work in a Lonely Era*, BlackRose Books.

HOWARD, W. (1920) 'Unrest amongst teachers'', *Socialist Review*, March 1920.

INTERNATIONAL LABOUR OFFICE (1989) *Report of an ILO Symposium on Collective Bargaining in Industrialised Market Economy Countries*, I.L.O., Geneva.

JARAUSCH, K.H. (1985) 'The crisis of the German Professions', *Journal of Contemporary History*, **20**, p. 394.

JOHNSON, R. (1986) 'The story so far: And further transformations?', in PUNTER, D. (Ed) *Introduction to Contemporary Cultural Studies*, London, Longman, pp. 277–313.

JOHNSON, R. (1989) 'Thatcherism and English education', *History of Education*, **18**, 2.

JONES, K. (1989) *Right Turn: The Conservative Revolution in Education*, London, Hutchinson Radius.

KEAN, H. (1990) *Deeds Not Words*, London, Pluto Press.

KEDWARD, R. and AUSTIN, R. (1985) *Vichy France and the Resistance*, London, Croom Helm.

KERCHNER, C. and MITCHELL, D. (1988) *The Changing Idea of a Teachers' Union*, London, Falmer Press.

KING, S. (1987) 'Feminists in teaching: The National Union of Women Teachers 1920–1940', in LAWN, M.A. and GRACE, G. (Eds) *Teachers: The Culture and Politics of Work*, London, Falmer Press.

KISCH, R. (1985) *The Days of the Good Soldier*, London, Journeyman Press.

KOCHAN, T.A., KATZ, H.C. and McKERSIE, R.B. (1986) *The Transformation of American Industrial Relations*, Basic Books, New York.

KOGAN, M. (1971) *Politics of Education*, Harmondsworth, Penguin.

LABOUR PARTY (1918) *Labour and the New Social Order*, LP.

LAW, J. (1994) *Organizing Modernity*, Oxford, Blackwell.

LAWN, M.A. (1983) 'Organised teachers and the Labour movement, 1900–1930', PhD thesis, Open University.

LAWN, M.A. (1985) 'Deeply tainted with socialism: The activities of the Teachers' Labour League in England and Wales in the 1920s', *History of Education Review*, **14**, 2, pp. 25–35.

LAWN, M.A. (1987a) *Servants of the State: The Contested Control of Teaching 1900–1930*, London, Falmer Press.

LAWN, M. (1987b) 'What is the teacher's job?: Work and welfare in elementary teaching 1940–1945', in LAWN, M.A. and GRACE, G. (Eds) *Teachers: The Culture and Politics of Work*, London, Falmer Press.

LAWN, M. (1988a) 'Skill in schoolwork: Work relations in the primary school', in OZGA, J. (Ed) *Schoolwork: Approaches to the Labour Process of Teaching*, Milton Keynes, Open University Press.

LAWN, M. (1988b) 'Democratic renewal in schools: A place for socio-technical change', in CARR, W. (Ed) *Quality in Education*, London, Falmer Press.

LAWN, M. (1989) 'The British way and purpose: The spirit of the age in curriculum history', *Journal of Curriculum Studies*, **21**, 2, pp. 113–28.

LAWN, M.A. (1991) 'The social construction of quality in teaching', in GRACE, G. and LAWN, M.A. (Eds) *Teacher Supply and Teacher Quality*, Clevedon, UK, Multilingual Matters.

LAWN, M. and OZGA, J. (1986) 'Unequal partners: Teachers under indirect rule', *British Journal of the Sociology of Education*, **7**, 2, pp. 225–38.

LAWN, M.A. and OZGA, J.T. (1988) 'Schoolwork: Interpreting the labour process in teaching', *British Journal of Sociology of Education*, **9**, 3, pp. 323–36.

LAWN, M. and WHITTY, G. (1992) 'England and Wales', in COOPER, B. (Ed) *Labor Relations in Education*, Westport, Conn, Greenwood Press.

LOUKES, H. (1956) *Secondary Modern*, London, George Harrap.

LUGARD, SIR F.D. (1923) *The Dual Mandate in British Tropical Africa*, London, Blackwood and Sons.

MANZER, R.M. (1970) *Teachers and Politics*, Manchester University Press.

MASS OBSERVATION ARCHIVE (1942) Observer F5065, Wartime Diary, University of Sussex.

MERCER, K. (1990) 'Welcome to the jungle', in RUTHERFORD, J. (Ed) *Identity*, London, Lawrence and Wishart.

MORGAN, G. (1986) *Images of Organization*, Beverley Hills, Sage.

MORTIMORE, P. MORTIMORE, J. and THOMAS, H. (1993) *The Innovative Uses of Non Teaching Staff in Primary and Secondary Schools*, London, DFE/HMSO.

MINISTRY OF EDUCATION (1947) *The New Secondary Education*, HMSO, London.

MINISTRY OF EDUCATION (1950) *Challenge and Response: An Account of the Emergency Scheme for the Training of Teachers*, London, HMSO.

MURRAH, A.V. (1929) *The School in the Bush*, London, Longman.

MURRAY, R. (1989) 'The State after Henry', in *Marxism Today*, May 1989.

NALT (1930) *Education: A Policy*, NALT.

NATIONAL PRIMARY CENTRE (NPC) (1989) *Effective Teaching*, Oxford, NPC.

NEILL, A.S. (1916) *A Dominie's Log*, Edinburgh, Herbert Jenkins.

NEILL, A.S. (1917) *A Dominie Dismissed*, Edinburgh, Herbert Jenkins.

NOVY, H. (1985) 'Army education, September 1941', in CALDER, A. and SHERIDAN, D. *Speak for Yourself: A Mass Observation Anthology*, London, Oxford University Press.

NUT (1929) *Hadow Report and After,* London, NUT.

NUT (1935) 'Memorandum of evidence to the Spens Committee', in RUBINSTEIN, D. and SIMON, B. (Eds) (1969) *The Evolution of the Comprehensive school 1926–1972,* London, RKP.

OZGA, J.T. (1987) 'Part of the union: School representatives and their work', in LAWN, M. and GRACE, G. (Eds) *Teachers: The Culture and Politics of Work,* London, Falmer Press.

OZGA, J.T. and LAWN, M.A. (1981) *Teachers, Professionalism and Class,* London, Falmer Press.

OZGA, J.T. and LAWN, M.A. (1981) 'Schoolwork: Interpreting the labour process of teaching', in *British Journal of Sociology of Education,* **9**, 3.

OTA, H. (1985) 'Political teacher unionism in Japan', in LAWN, M. *The Politics of Teacher Unionism,* London, Croom Helm.

PARTRIDGE, J. (1966) *Life in a Secondary Modern School,* London, Pelican.

POLLARD, A. and TANN, S. (1987) *Reflective Teaching in the Primary School,* London, Cassell.

PERCY, LORD E.P. (1922) 'The civil service and foreign policy', in *Society of Civil Servants: The Development of the Civil Service King and Sons,* London, Kings and Sons, pp. 37–59.

PERCY LORD E.P. (1958) *Some Memories,* London, Eyre and Spottiswoode.

PRED, A. (1995) *Recognizing European Modernities,* London, Routledge.

PUBLIC RECORDS OFFICE (1923) File ED/24/1757 *Drift of Teachers Towards the Labour Party.*

PUBLIC RECORDS OFFICE (1920–26) file ED/241753 *Teachers and the Oath of Allegiance.*

PUBLIC RECORDS OFFICE (1926–34) file ED/241761 *Political Activities of Teachers 1926–1934.*

REPORT OF THE CONSULTATIVE COMMITTEE ON THE EDUCATION OF THE ADOLESCENT (1926) (*Hadow Report*), London, HMSO.

RHODES, G. (1981) *Inspectorates in British Government: Law Enforcement and Standards of Efficiency,* London, Allen and Unwin.

RICHMOND, W.K. (1945) *Education in England,* London, Pelican.

SARAN, R. (1989) 'The politics behind Burnham', Sheffield Polytechnic.

SAMUELS, R. (1983) 'The middle class between the wars', *New Socialist,* Pts. 1–3.

SAYER, A. (1989) 'Post-Fordism in question', in *International Journal of Urban and Regional Research,* 13, 4.

SCARLYN WILSON, N. (Ed) (1948) *Education in the Forces 1939–1946: The Civilian Contribution,* London, Evans Bros.

SCHEIN, E.H. (Ed) (1987) *The Art of Managing Human Resources,* Oxford, Oxford University Press.

SELBY-BIGGE, SIR L.A. (1927) *The Board of Education,* London, Putnam and Sons.

SHERINGTON, G. (1981) *English Education, Social Change and War 1911–1920,* Manchester, Manchester University Press.

SILVER, H. (1992) 'Knowing and not knowing in the history of education', in *History of Education*, **121**, 1, pp. 97–108.

SIMON, B. (1974) *The Politics of Educational Reform, 1920–1940*, London, Lawrence and Wishart.

SIMON, B. (1985) 'Why no pedagogy in England?', in *Does Education Matter?*, London, Lawrence and Wishart.

STEWART, J. (1991) 'Meeting needs in the 90s: The future of public services and the challenge for trade unions', London, Institute of Public Policy Research.

STOER, S. (1985) 'The April revolution and teacher trade unionism, in Portugal,' in LAWN, M. (Ed) *Politics of Teacher Unionism*, London, Croom Helm.

TAWNEY, R.H. (1921) *The Acquisitive Society*, London, Bell.

TOURAINE, A. (1981) *The Voice and the Eye: An Analysis of Social Movements*, Cambridge, Cambridge University Press.

TOWNSEND, J. (1966) *The Young Devils: Experiences of a Schoolteacher*, London, Chatto and Windus.

TROPP, A. (1957) *The Schoolteachers*, London, Heinemann.

TYACK, D. (1990) 'Restructuring in historical perspective: Tinkering towards utopia', in *Teachers College Record*, **92**, 2.

VAN HUUTEN, D.R. (1987) 'The political economy and technical control of work humanization in Sweden during the 1970s and 1980s', in *Work and Occupations*, **14**, 4, pp. 483–513.

WEBB, B. (1915) 'English teachers and their professional organisations', in *New Statesman*, 25 September.

WEBB, S. (1918) *The Teacher in Politics*, **187**, London, Fabian Society.

WELLS, D.M. (1997) 'Empty promises: Quality of working life programs and the Labour movement', *Monthly Review Press*.

WELLS, H.G. (1908) *New Worlds for Old*, London, Constable.

WHITE, J. (1975) 'The end of the compulsory curriculum', in *Curriculum: The Doris Lee Lectures Studies in Education*, **2**, Institute of Education, University of London.

WILLIAMS, F. (1947) *Fifty Years March*, Odhams.

WOODS, P. (1984) 'Teacher, self and curriculum', in GOODSON, I. and BALL, S. (Eds) *Defining the Curriculum: Histories and Ethnographies*, Lewes, Falmer Press.

Index

accountability, 139
accountants, 93
administration, 25–8, 35, 66
adult education programmes, 43–5, 48–53
Africa, 27
anarchy, 53
Army Bureau of Current Affairs (ABCA),
    43, 48–53, 56, 76
Army education, 43–7, 56–60, 67
Army School of Education, 52
assessment, 89–90, 112, 130
Association of Teachers and Lecturers
    (ATL), 136
attendance, 37
Audit Commission, 115
autonomy, 21

Baldwin, S., 22, 23, 93
Barber, M., 124
beliefs, 15
Beveridge Report, 55–6
Blishen, E., 82, 85
Blumer, H., 59
Board of Education, 21–3, 26–8, 63, 65
boarding schools, 39
Bolshevization, 25
boundaries, 14–16
Boy Scouts, 37
Brains Trust, 76
Braithwaite, E.R., 81
Britain, 13–14, 19, 43–60, 122–6, 130–5,
    140–50
budgets, 130–1
Burgundy Book, 133
Burnham Panel, 22, 32, 90–1, 95–6, 102,
    112, 123, 132–3
Burston Strike School, 38

Calder, A., 43
Catholic Church, 12

Central Advisory Council for Education
    in England, 68
centralization, 22, 96
Centre for Policy Studies, 71
Chamberlain, N., 22, 23
child-centred education, 40
Christian Socialism, 38
Christianity, 76, 78
church schools, 37
Churchill, W., 22, 23, 55
citizenship, 9, 17, 50, 53–4, 79
    army education, 52
    current affairs, 47
    demobilization, 44–5
    project method, 77
    secondary modern schools, 82
civil liberties, 17–18, 37
civil servants, 25–6, 66, 96
class, 24, 38, 41, 64–5, 70
classrooms, 14–15, 18, 37, 71, 73–88,
    140
cleaning services, 93
clubs, 78
co-education, 39, 85
Cole, G.D.H., 34, 35–6
Coleg Harlech, 52
collective bargaining, 95, 109, 112–13,
    123–4, 131–2
    decentralization, 134
    future trends, 137
    militancy, 127
    role, 126
colonial government, 21, 23, 27–9, 93–4,
    126
communism, 15, 24, 33, 39–40, 46, 104
comprehensive schools, 104, 105–6
compulsory attendance, 37
comradeship, 38, 48
conferences, 125–6
conflict, 124, 125